STOP OVERTHINKING

HOW TO OVERCOME NEGATIVE THINKING, PROCRASTINATION, ANXIETY, AND OTHER NEGATIVE EMOTIONS. HOW TO INCREASE SELF-ESTEEM, SELF-CONFIDENCE, EMOTIONAL INTELLIGENCE AND PRODUCTIVITY.

Mark Mind

MARK MIND

© **Copyright 2020 - All rights reserved.**

The content contained within this book may not be reproduced, duplicated or transmitted without direct written permission from the author or the publisher.

Under no circumstances will any blame or legal responsibility be held against the publisher, or author, for any damages, reparation, or monetary loss due to the information contained within this book. Either directly or indirectly.

Legal Notice: This book is copyright protected. This book is only for personal use. You cannot amend, distribute, sell, use, quote or paraphrase any part, or the content within this book, without the consent of the author or publisher.

Disclaimer Notice: Please note the information contained within this document is for educational and entertainment purposes only. All effort has been executed to present accurate, up to date, and reliable, complete information. No warranties of any kind are declared or implied. Readers acknowledge that the author is not engaging in the rendering of legal, financial, medical or professional advice. The content within this book has been derived from various sources. Please consult a licensed professional before attempting any techniques outlined in this book.

By reading this document, the reader agrees that under no circumstances is the author responsible for any losses, direct or indirect, which are incurred as a result of the use of information contained within this document, including, but not limited to, — errors, omissions, or inaccuracies.

Table of Contents

Introduction 6

Chapter 1 - Crucial Tips To Solving Overthinking 12

Chapter 2 - The Number One Most Important Thing To Understand If You Want To Be Happy In This World: Mastering Your Mind 22

Chapter 3 - How To Improve Your Performance In Work? 30

Chapter 4 - How To Increase Your Productivity? 38

Chapter 5 - How To Improve Your Mood, No Matter What Are Your Circumstances? 46

Chapter 6 - Simple Steps To Remove Negative Influences From Your Life 52

Chapter 7 - How To Develop Self-Confidence 60

Chapter 8 - Develop The Habits Of Successful People 64

Chapter 9 - Why And How To Stop Procrastination In Your Life 72

Chapter 10 - Ways To Avoid Decision Fatigue 80

Chapter 11 - Challenging Your Thoughts 86

Chapter 12 - Mental Clutter 94

Chapter 13 - Embracing Mindfulness As An Efficient Alternative To Overthinking 104

Chapter 14 - Effects Of Overthinking 114

Chapter 15 - How To Stop Overthinking With Positive Self-Talk 122

Chapter 16 - How To Solve Worry Problems? 132

Chapter 17 - Reframing Your Negative Thoughts 140

Chapter 18 - How To Use Meditation To Deal With Overthinking? 146

Chapter 19 - Returning To Self-Care 154

Chapter 20 - The Key To Feeling Good 162

Chapter 21 - Self-Discipline 170

Chapter 22 - Goal Setting 178

Chapter 23 - Forgetting Your Past 186

Chapter 24 - Deliberate Thinking 193

Chapter 25 - Exercises That Help Positive Thinking 202

Chapter 26 - How To Make Important Decisions Today? 208

Conclusion 216

Introduction

The biggest cause of unhappiness is overthinking.

A big gap exists between deliberating and solving problems. Some often suggest that women are more likely to overthink than men, but the truth is that no one manages to avoid overthinking; it is something everyone does.

A therapist meets with thousands of individuals in their office daily, many of whom are searching for help in dealing with overthinking. Many often complain about their inability to relax. They feel that their brain is constantly preoccupied with worries and negative thoughts, and, as a result, they feel so much anxiety that they can't rest. Some complaint about the fact that they focus excessively on how much better their lives would be without the mistakes they have made.

There is a strong connection between overthinking and mental health problems, such as anxiety and depression. Those suffering from overthinking might not even notice the decline in their mental health because they are so preoccupied and worried; they are not living in the mindfully. Such individuals might feel that their overthinking is healthy and useful, and without it, some horrible calamity might happen.

But the truth is just the opposite. Overthinking increases the chances of feeling lost, anxious, and miserable. It can also lead to resentment and anger that clouds your judgment and makes it hard for you to make the right decisions. This state is often referred to as analysis paralysis.

Overthinking keeps reminding you of things you can't control, such as your failure. There are basically two forms of overthinking, namely: an excessive rumination on the past and worrying excessively about future events. These preoccupations prevent you from making progress in your life. There is a clear difference between overthinking, self-reflection, and problem-solving.

How is overthinking different from problem-solving? There is a clear difference between problem-solving and overthinking. When problem-solving, your goal is to solve an underlying problem. Overthinkers dwell more on the problems themselves than possible solutions to their problems.

How about self-reflection? Is it the same as overthinking? No! Self-reflection has a definite purpose; it helps you discover new things about yourself, your condition, and your situation.

What's the bottom line? While you are overthinking, you're not productive. However, self-reflection and problem-solving help you create solutions and recognize behaviors that may be holding you back.

We all have a tendency to overthink. Being aware of this fact makes it easier to change. And the first step involves identifying the damage caused by overthinking.

The idea that overthinking stops bad things from happening is a subconscious perception nurtured by many; they feel that the failure to ruminate over past events will precipitate some sort of unforeseen calamity. Research indicates that overthinking is not healthy and will impact our lives negatively.

If you notice the tendency to become enmeshed in overthinking, don't despair. You can use the strategies below to get back your energy, time, and brainpower.

From proper time scheduling to thought substitution, here are several exercises that will boost your mental strength and help you stop overthinking everything.

If you are an overthinker, you limit your chances of becoming successful in life. It will prevent you from reaching your goals and make your life miserable.

Why have an uplifting standpoint in life, since you can? Since there's a great deal in it for you. That is the reason. Keep in mind, positive reasoning is believing that is naturally advantageous. This is the thing that makes it 'positive' in any case.

You've just observed the 10,000-foot view perspective on the three essential advantages: positive reasoning causes you to accomplish something you need, encourages you to feel better (or if nothing else better), and it's helpful and quickly improves your life somehow or another.

Be that as it may, you can burrow down further to identify progressively specific advantages that are likewise worth increasing in value. In view of this, here are a few advantages of reasoning all the more emphatically:

More achievement: having more vitality, progressively confidence, and increasingly self-assurance prompts more achievement

Better rest and wellbeing: increasingly quiet, positive feelings imply less unpleasant, negative feelings that can negatively affect your body; the outcome is you appreciate the medical advantages of positive reasoning, including better nature of rest

A progressively beneficial life: the more you increase the value of your life with positive reasoning, the more advantageous life is for you

More noteworthy certainty: the more you trust you can accomplish things (a typical type of positive reasoning), the more self-assurance you have

More satisfaction and happiness: the more positive worth that you find in life, the more joyful you become, and the more you appreciate life

Feeling more grounded: as your certainty and confidence increments because of positive reasoning, you likewise feel more grounded and all the more dominant

More vitality: positive reasoning frequently persuades and stimulates you to accomplish things

More genuine feelings of serenity: the better you feel by and large with positive reasoning, the more significant serenity you have

Higher confidence: the more worth you find in yourself with positive reasoning, the higher your feeling of self-esteem

Increasingly agreeable cooperation with others: the more you appreciate life and worth yourself, the more you will in general appreciate social connections

More noteworthy clearness of brain: since you have a decision, it bodes well to think in legitimate, adequate positive ways that advantage you as opposed to in negative manners that hurt you; this is an advantage of positive reasoning great worth considering

Does thinking positive have any kind of effect?

Completely. You simply figured out how you can profit by positive intuition from numerous points of view, so sure reasoning truly works for improving your life.

The most significant inquiry, at the present time, is this: would you like to think positive contemplations and turned into an increasingly positive scholar?

This is on the grounds that the most significant factor for turning into an increasingly positive mastermind is to just need to think all the more emphatically, and to be definitive about making a move to think progressively positive considerations, paying little mind to whether any other individual needs you to think all the more decidedly or not.

With this lucidity of the brain, you are as of now well on your approach to growing increasingly positive perspectives about things.

Along these lines, if you have just realized what positive reasoning is, your following stage is to study how to think all the more emphatically and how to remain positive regardless of the conditions.

Chapter 1
Crucial Tips to Solving Overthinking

How to form good habits?

Have you, at any point, asked why a few people appear to complete difficult tasks to such a large extent? When the state, "I am going to…" begin working out, eat healthily, get sorted out, read more, and so forth, you realize that they're going to get it going. Be that s it may, when you attempt to follow comparable objectives, it is an alternate story.

You may most likely adhere to them for some time, yet at that point, incidentally, you generally lose your inspiration and quit.

At the point when that happens on enough occasions, it is anything but difficult to get disappointed and debilitated. Be that as it may, making and continuing great habits do not need to be so troublesome and difficult. Actually, it very well may be very simple. Furthermore, even a great deal of fun. Here are the means by which to grow great habits and ensure they remain as such:

1. Observe your small wins

In case you are similar to the vast majority, you are greatly improved at thumping yourself for an awful execution than you are at compensating yourself for a decent one. With regards to overseeing ourselves, for reasons unknown, we appear to favor the carrot. Furthermore, that is a disgrace since research has demonstrated that commending your advancement is significant for your inspiration.

Each time you remunerate yourself for gaining ground, regardless of how little, you enact the reward hardware in your brain. That discharges some key synthetic substances which make you experience sentiments of accomplishment and pride. These feelings, thus, enable you to make a move and make greater triumphs later on. Along these lines, compensate yourself for each positive development, regardless of how little they happen to be.

2. Encircle yourself with supporters

The general population around us has a shockingly enormous effect on our conduct. One investigation demonstrated that on the off chance that you have a companion who winds up fat, your danger of weight increments by in excess of fifty percent regardless of whether your companion lives many miles away.

Other research has demonstrated that we will, in general, feel a similar way, and receive similar objectives, as the general population we invest the most energy with. In this way, one approach to drastically expand your odds of progress is to ensure you have the correct individuals in your corner. On the off chance that you need to make sound propensities, however, the entirety of your companions are undesirable, it is an ideal opportunity to make some new companions.

What's more, on the off chance that you need to make enormous things occur in your life yet you are encompassed with worrywarts who drag you down, it is a great opportunity to make a care group who moves you and lifts you back up when you come up short. You are normal of the five individuals you invest the most energy with, so be particular about them.

3. Get hooked on your habit

Have you, at any point, seeing that it is so difficult to relinquish an undertaking when you have put a great deal of exertion into it? We can utilize this inclination to further our potential benefit by utilizing the "Do not break the chain" methodology.

This is an extremely sharp procedure you can use to make a visual reminder of how much exertion you have put resources into your propensity. You will likely find that the more extended the chain develops, the harder you will battle to prop it up. In this way, get a schedule, put a marker by it, and get the opportunity to chip away at your propensity. Your solitary employment next is to not break the chain.

4. Structure your environment

From various perspectives, your condition drives your conduct. Have you at any point strolled into your kitchen, detected a plate of treats on the counter, and eaten them since they were before you? The thought is that every single one of your propensities requires a specific measure of vitality to complete. Furthermore, the more enactment vitality it needs, the more uncertain you will be to finish and do it.

Suppose you need to peruse more books; however, you more often than not end up sitting in front of the TV. What you have to do is:

• Increase the enactment vitality of your undesired propensity (sitting in front of the TV). For instance, taking the TV remote in the next room.

• Decrease the enactment vitality of your ideal propensity (perusing books). For instance, putting an incredible book beside your lounge love seat.

5. Change your mindset

At whatever point you are making another propensity, receive a researcher and subject mindset. Consider all that you complete a social examination where every mishap gives important information to your subsequent stage. Move your consideration away from the long-haul objective and rather center around appearing and doing your propensity each and every day.

6. Pre-commit to your habit

Envision it is 5:00 am, and your caution goes off. Inside seconds, your arrangement of setting off to the exercise center before work is in peril as your brain begins to think.

"Well, I'm quite drained. I wonder if it is even beneficial to work out when I'm this worn out. I could go to the rec. center after work. Or then again, I could go to the rec. center tomorrow first thing. Definitely, I'll hit the rest catch."

Abruptly, returning to rest won't be such an engaging choice. By pre-submitting thusly, you can include an additional layer of responsibility that makes you push through notwithstanding when it is hard.

How to prevent yourself from falling into the trap of overthinking

Here are practices to help you stop overthinking.

Become aware of your inclination to overthinking

Before one can address or cope with her habit of overthinking, they need to be aware of when they are doing so. They will become aware of it when they pick up on the signs. Even a person's lips signal the person when they are buried in thoughts because the lips will tend to feel dry. Anytime when a person finds themselves doubting or feeling stressed or anxious, they can step back and look at the situation, and how they are responding to it.

Think of what can go right instead of what can go wrong

What? Is it good to prepare yourself for anything by imagining the worst-case scenarios? That may work in the movies, but it is not a philosophy for a meaningful life. In most cases, emotions of fear bring about overthinking. When a person focuses on all the things that could go wrong, they may become paralyzed in their thinking. As soon as a person senses that they are going down an overthinking spiral, they need to stop. Instead, they can visualize all the things that can go right and maintain that pattern of thinking.

Dive into pleasure and happiness

Sometimes it is helpful for a person to have a way to distract themselves with happy, positive, and healthy alternatives. Any experience that can bring happy thoughts is worth spending time on. Activities like meditation, dancing, exercise, how to play a musical instrument, drawing, painting, and knitting can distract a person from overthinking.

Similarly, a person can opt to go on nature walks, take a swim, create a new recipe, bake, eat out with friends, or watch a movie. A person can find happiness in the simplest pleasures. Just be happy, and you can live to a hundred!

Stop expecting, or waiting for perfection

For overthinkers who are waiting to see perfection in the world around them, they should stop doing so. Every person has their idea of what perfection looks like. Therefore, perfection will never be a blueprint for anyone or anything. Being ambitious is a great thing, but aiming for perfection is impractical, incapacitating, and unrealistic. That is because it simply does not exist in the real world.

The moment a person starts to think that certain things need to be perfect that is the moment they should remind themselves that waiting for perfection is not as constructive as making progress.

Change how you view fear

Often a person is afraid because they have failed in the past, or they are fearful of trying or is overanalyzing some other failure. If anything, failure is not a stop sign. Instead, it is merely a way of telling someone to look to the other side.

In such cases, a person needs to remind themselves that just because things did not work the first time, it does not mean that things will not work a second time.

A person should remember that each opportunity is a different chance to have a new beginning.

Put things into perspective

It is always easy for one to make issues more significant and more harmful than necessary.

Just because your workmate did not say hello to you when you greeted them in the morning, does not mean that they are mad at you, or are putting you off. Maybe if you looked at your colleague more intently, you would notice that they were wearing their earphones!

The next time a person catches themselves making a mountain out of a molehill, they should ask themselves whether the issue will matter in five years, or a week.

Realize that you cannot predict the future

No one can. Therefore, all the time a person has is the present time. Sometimes people become bent on living their present time in view of their future. The truth is, no one can predict how things will happen in the next hour, let alone in the future. People can have ideas, but no one can know for sure.

When a person spends her present time worrying about the future, they are robbing themselves of the present time. Spending time thinking of one's future is not productive. Instead, they should spend that time on things that bring them joy.

Appreciate your best

The fear that holds overthinking is often based on the feeling that one is not good, smart, diligent, or dedicated enough. In life, there never comes a time when people feel that they have reached their full potential.

Therefore, people learn to give their best effort to the tasks that they have to do at each level. In other words, being the best person one can be is a matter of choice and effort. Once a person gives their best effort, they should accept it and know that while success may depend in part on some things that they cannot control, they did the best that they could.

Be grateful

A person cannot have a grateful and regretful thought simultaneously. Therefore, why should they not choose to spend the time positively?

Consequently, every evening, one should create a habit of listing down all the things that they are grateful for. The person should then find a friend with whom they can share the list. In that way, both people can learn how to share and be grateful for positive things and experiences around them.

One needs to form a habit of appreciating the good, however small that may be. Little good things eventually become great things!

Chapter 2
The Number One Most Important Thing to Understand If You Want To Be Happy in This World: Mastering Your Mind

You may struggle with your thoughts. Often, we let our thoughts control us, choose our actions, and bring us down. However, you must be able to control your thoughts if you want to be happy. Mastering your mind will help you to become the leader of your emotions instead of feeling the need to react to and follow them. You will be able to focus more clearly on what matters to you instead of being swayed by your current thoughts. When you become a master of your mind, you will be able to face any situation that comes with you, and you will be much stronger overall.

To master your mind, you must learn how to control your thoughts. You must be able to take control of your thinking instead of letting it take control of you. You must also learn how to ride your emotional waves. Instead of letting your emotions control your actions, you must allow your emotions to happen naturally. Manipulating your mindset can also help you, as it will allow you to control the way you think. It's critical for you to not allow outside influences to destroy your thoughts. You are the one and only master of your mind. Don't let others bring you down.

Controlling your thinking

You are constantly thinking. Your brain is always shifting to a new subject; there's always something new to be thinking about. Often, our minds wander to places that we wish they wouldn't. It would make it so much easier if you were just able to control how you thought, right? Well, it's possible. Instead of dwelling on our worries, overthinking every situation, and wasting our time on thoughts that we wish we wouldn't, we may practice taking control over our thoughts. With time and practice, you can easily shift your thinking to more pleasant and productive thoughts. You may find yourself becoming stressed out as a result of your thoughts. However, you can help shift that so that you think better. You may shift your thinking to more important and meaningful thoughts as well. Instead of letting your mind wander, you can control where your mind goes. You may think about what you want to so that you have the desired reaction to your thoughts.

To control your thoughts, you must be able to stop unwanted thoughts. Perhaps you are thinking something that stresses you out, makes you sad or causes frustration. To do so, you must catch yourself when you are thinking one of these thoughts and realize what the thought is and what effect it is having on you. When you feel yourself becoming upset, take a moment to reflect on yourself. What are you feeling at the moment? Are you stressed, mad, frustrated, sad, disappointed, anxious, or something else? Every feeling that you experience is caused by a thought that you have. Take a step back and identify what is causing that specific feeling. You may have to write down every single thought that you have or really scan your brain to determine what you're thinking.

After this, identify the further causes and effects. Why does that make you feel that way? Is it because of a negative event that happened similar to that? Did somebody else give you a bad feeling about an upcoming event? Determine why exactly you feel that way about whatever it is. There is almost always more than just the surface-level emotion and reasoning that is affecting you.

Once you have identified what caused this emotion, let it out. You may rant inside your head. You may choose to write it all down. You may even talk to somebody that you trust. Regardless, you should let out the emotion somehow; it is healthier to do so than to suppress your emotions. If you haven't dealt with a former problem, you will need to now. Perhaps you are nervous about an upcoming interview because the last one you went to didn't work out well. Your brain will return to that disappointment until you have dealt with it and moved on. You must be able to separate the new situation from the old one. Those negative thoughts should not interfere with that. By dealing with the negative thoughts associated with that, you will remove yourself from that and be able to move on from the pain. You will also be able to get this mental image out of your mind.

Riding your emotional waves

Emotions are just like waves. They come and go, and they're always changing. They go in different directions, have different intensities, and can be very powerful. Waves can be dangerous. If you go against the wave, you can be pushed against, pulled down, and even drown. This is similar to your emotions. If you try to suppress them or fight against them, you will not win. The emotions will take over and leave you feeling overwhelmed and defeated. However, it's possible for you to learn how to "surf" your emotions and use them to your advantage. Riding your waves instead of fighting against them can prove highly beneficial to you.

You must be able to anticipate the waves. Recognize that they will always come, and there is nothing that you can do to stop them. However, you may deal with them differently. A wave doesn't seem as overwhelming if you learn how to ride it. It only seems massive when you are about to be overcome by it. Understand that emotions will come and go and develop an appreciation for your emotions. This is what makes you yourself. There will be different emotions at different times and with different intensities.

You must be able to observe the wave before it comes. Acknowledge its existence and what type of wave it is. There will be different waves, and you must be able to identify them and differentiate them. Recognize what type of emotion you are feeling. Do this without adding in your judgment. You must recognize that it is a part of who you are, but it doesn't define who you are. Every wave will be different, and you must be able to realize that. Determine how intense the wave is, as that will determine how you may best ride it.

You must be willing to ride the wave. Instead of letting it drown you, simply experience it. Realize that the wave will come and go. Just let it happen. Experience the emotion. Don't let it overpower you. If you fight against the emotion, you will only feel like you are drowning. Instead, let the wave happen. Realize that it won't last forever and riding it out will really help you. You may let yourself go through the stages of the wave so that you can experience it. You may just take some time to let it happen and do whatever feels natural.

Remember that there are always new waves coming. The wave that you are currently experiencing will not last forever. It will be replaced by a new wave. You will not be stuck on the same wave for the rest of your life. It will, in fact, make it easier for you to move onto the next wave if you learn to ride the current wave out. You may start to develop an excitement for the waves that you experience. It can be like a game for you. There is always a new wave coming; what will the next one be? Develop an excitement and appreciation for the variety of emotions that you experience. Don't view your emotions as either positive or negative. They are all part of the experience of life. You will have an emotion that you are riding right now, but that doesn't mean that you will be riding the same one next week, tomorrow, or even an hour from now. Be open to all of the emotions that you experience, as they will all be temporary. Experiencing one emotion may give you an even greater appreciation for another. Accept the wide variety of emotional waves that you ride.

Manipulating your mindset

Your mindset makes a huge difference in your way of thinking, your amount of motivation, your productivity, and your emotions. When you are able to shift your mindset to the one that you desire, you will be able to accomplish more and feel better. It is necessary for you to reframe your mindset so that you can accomplish your goals. Instead of reacting to everything, you must shift your way to respond to life. Obstacles are not what define you; it is how you overcome those obstacles that make you who you are and define how successful you will be.

One way to shift your mindset is to alter the way you view yourself. Instead of letting your mistakes define you, focus on your success and your potential for greater success. You must be able to be positive with yourself. Recognize that there is always room for improvement, and mistakes will always occur. New opportunities will always arise, and not every opportunity is meant for you. Realize that some missed opportunities will allow you the chance to experience others that you wouldn't have been able to otherwise. In general, you must shift your mindset regarding yourself. Remind yourself that you are capable of anything that you set your mind to, and you will be able to accomplish your goals.

You must also shift your mindset pertaining to outside situations. You may be unhappy with your current life at the moment, but you must be able to appreciate all of life: the good and bad. Shift your mindset to a growth mindset. There is always room for improvement, and you can make changes to your life to improve it. Never sell yourself short, as you always have the potential to make your life closer to the ideal image that you have for yourself.

Control your own thoughts

We often let others control our thoughts. We can allow others to change our way of viewing the world and have them alter our emotions. You may be in a good mood, and one person may completely change your day (for better or for worse). It's important to not allow this to happen. You must be able to take full responsibility for your thoughts and emotions, and you shouldn't let others change that. Stay in control of your own thoughts. Although it's important to allow yourself to learn and grow from others, you must be able to still remain the ultimate master of your thoughts.

Regularly check in with yourself. Determine if how you are feeling is the result of someone else. If so, take a moment to separate yourself from the situation and reflect. Remember that everyone is entitled to their own thoughts. If someone tries to bring you down, respect that they may not be having the best day and handle your own emotions yourself. Stand up for yourself and your emotions. Avoid those who tend to focus on negative thoughts, drama, or the like. Stand up for your own beliefs and don't let others change those or bring you down.

Chapter 3

How to Improve Your Performance in Work?

Stress and work

Stress and productivity affect each other. When one suffers, the other one also suffers. This can have a huge impact on you at work. You can find it difficult to accomplish what you need when you have stress bringing you down. You may also find it difficult to not feel stressed when you are having an unproductive day. Because of this, you must learn how to properly deal with stress at work so that you can remain productive and accomplish what you need to throughout your day at work, reducing stress.

When you're at home, it may be a bit easier to manage your stress. You may have loved ones (people or pets) around, and they can support you. There is food available, and you can relax in an area that you choose. You may not have to worry as much about anybody needing you to do anything, and it can be easier to destress. At work, however, there are others around that will need help from you. You will have a boss supervising you (or you'll have to set a good example for those that you are the boss of). There are others around you that may not be your favorite people. You may also be unsatisfied with your job. There are a lot of possible ways that you may become stressed out at work. You must know how to manage this stress to make your workday better for yourself.

When you feel stressed at work, you may start becoming overwhelmed, anxious, irritable, unmotivated, or fatigued. It may become hard for you to focus on your work. When this happens, it's important to take a small break if possible. If it is possible, you may take a few minutes to go to the bathroom just so that you may take a bit of time away from your current task. You may even walk around or do something for a bit to distract yourself. If you can't take a break, at least take a few breaths. Distract yourself by thinking of something that calms you down and makes you happy. You may try to talk to others, whether those are customers or coworkers. Try to reach out to others at work so that you have people to support you and to socialize with. By having people at work that you enjoy talking to, you can enjoy your job much more.

Remember to take care of your body. When you don't sleep properly, you will lack the energy you need to stay focused. Always eat a good breakfast and remember to pack food for work. If you eat your meals at work, pack something nutritious and filling. Don't forget to have snacks and water available to you, too.

You may also leave earlier in the mornings. This will give you some extra time to get there in case there is traffic or anything else. It will also give you a bit of time to mentally prepare before work. You may make any plans for the day and schedule what needs to be scheduled. This is also a time to plan your breaks and what you'll do during your breaks. Remember not to over-commit yourself, as it will only wear you down.

Habits for increasing productivity

As you've learned, increasing your productivity is crucial to your success. It's necessary for reducing stress and getting more done at work. You'll feel much better when you increase your productivity. You'll also be able to get more done in a smaller amount of time. This means that you can meet more people, go to more places, make more money, accomplish more goals, and achieve more of what you want. What's to lose? Of course, you may lose out on some of life's distractions and wasted moments. But what are you waiting for? Tomorrow never comes, and it's important to live in the moment and enjoy it as much as you possibly can instead of letting life pass before your eyes. The following are some helpful habits that you can implement so that you can increase your productivity.

One way is to track yourself. On your phone, you may be able to track how often you use certain apps. However, you should be able to do this in real life. Often, we don't even realize how we're spending our time. By scrupulously tracking your time, even if it's only for a bit, you'll learn how to better gauge the passing of time. For a week, have a clock ready and write down every single thing that you do. You may try this at work. Set up a place to write, and track everything you do. You may even do this for every hour of work that you do. However, the more detailed it is, the more that you'll learn from yourself and understand your habits. Instead of having a specific time to write down what you're doing, you may just write down whenever you change what you're doing. The example shows the tasks completed every hour, which can help you to understand how much you truly accomplish in a day.

By doing this, you may realize that you accomplish more in a day than you think you do. If this is the case, you can celebrate your success and work on improving yourself even more. Is there room for more improvement? If you find yourself accomplishing less than you thought you did or know that is possible for yourself, work on fixing one area at a time.

Eliminating distractions

From the notes about yourself that you made, you may identify what distracts you. By writing down what you get distracted by, you can make it much easier for yourself. Recognizing what distracts you is the first step to eliminating distractions from your life. When you can recognize what distracts you and catch yourself when you get distracted, you can reduce and eliminate distractions from your life, helping you to accomplish more instead of getting caught up in the distractions.

You should work in an environment that helps you to get more done, not one that distracts you. If you can eliminate what physically distracts you, it can be easier to get work done. At the end of each day, make sure that you clean up after yourself so that you don't have a huge pile of clutter to greet you at the beginning of each day. Staying organized and having a system for your items can help you to feel less overwhelmed. You'll also be able to focus on what matters. Turn off notifications from your phone, computer, and other devices that will distract you. You may even uninstall apps or put a block on them so that you aren't tempted to use them during work. Get rid of any distracting items that you may have. Typically, bright colors can be distracting and will catch your attention. By working in a place that you can focus on, you'll feel much better.

Eliminate potential bodily distractions. Keep snacks and water handy in case you get hungry and thirsty. This will save you the time that it takes to go get these items. Remember to get a proper amount of sleep so that you aren't tired. When you're tired, you won't have the energy to focus and be productive. Go to the bathroom before starting tasks and while on breaks. If you have to use the bathroom in the middle of working, remind yourself to get back on task instead of prolonging your break. You must take breaks, but it's also important to be able to regain your focus after taking a break. Otherwise, you can spend more of your time taking breaks instead of working. This is not a good way to be productive and accomplish what you want to.

Priorities and procrastination

To be productive, you need to eliminate procrastination and learn how to prioritize. Procrastination can really get you down and stop you from achieving your goals. However, you can eliminate procrastination by implementing a few habits into your life. You may also cut out some bad habits that serve as aids of procrastination. Prioritizing your tasks will also really help you to get done what you need to first. You will be able to focus on accomplishing what matters first instead of letting yourself get distracted by what doesn't. For this reason, procrastination and prioritizing go hand-in-hand. When you learn to prioritize, you are eliminating your procrastination.

Often, we tend to procrastinate without even realizing it. You may complete tasks that aren't as important or urgent instead of completing tasks that are more important and need to get done quicker. For instance, you may need to work on cleaning the house and scheduling a doctor's appointment for your medical issue. The house is important, as it needs to be clean so that you're healthy and happy. The doctor's appointment is urgent, as you must go to take care of your health. Instead of doing these tasks, which are the most important to you, you may find yourself doing everything but these tasks. You may go to the post office, shop for things you don't need, talk to friends and family, and do other unimportant tasks. When you look back at it, you had a productive day! You accomplished a lot and were able to get a lot done. However, you weren't accomplishing what you were supposed to be doing. It's important to realize that priorities only matter if you stick to them. It's possible to procrastinate and still get things done. You must learn how to truly avoid procrastination and follow your priorities.

The best way to do so is by utilizing to-do lists. Make a to-do list for the next day every night. This way, you'll focus on what actually needs to get done instead of what you want to get done. Come up with 1-3 IBU (important, big, and urgent) items for your list. These are the super important tasks for yourself. If you only accomplish these and absolutely nothing else, you'll be happy with your day. You can then jot down other, less-important tasks as well. These tasks, however, you can only work on if you've already accomplished your IBU tasks. This will help you to focus on what matters instead of getting caught up in what doesn't. It can also help you to split up the bigger tasks. If you find yourself becoming overwhelmed by everything you need to do, split up your tasks into smaller tasks.

You may also put yourself on a timer. Give yourself a set amount of time to work and a set amount of time for a break. Perhaps you work for 45 minutes and take 15-minute breaks. This means that you're working for 75% of each hour. Experiment and see what works.

Stress has a huge impact on your life. It can especially have an impact on your productivity. It can be really difficult to get things done when you're feeling stressed, which is why it's so important to learn how to properly manage your stress. When you're stressed, your productivity decreases. When your productivity decreases, your stress will increase. They have an inverse effect on each other. It's important to become more productive so that you may prevent and reduce stress for yourself.

Chapter 4

How to Increase Your Productivity?

One of the biggest problems with overthinking is that it leads to procrastination. In fact, the whole point of the brain for causing anxiety is to push you into inactivity. It wants you to stick to a corner so that the risk can be minimized It is no way to live in this world where your contribution matters.

Procrastination is one of the most common side-effects of overthinking. It keeps you in a never-ending loop of thinking that has no scope of action. Your mind can keep forming strategies and then discarding them after a point to form newer and better ones. This process can be continued until the end of time.

What you really need is a plan to break the chain of thoughts and get into action. The longer you keep thinking, the harder it will get to stop overthinking about it. Even the best strategies in the world can get washed down the drain if they are not put into action.

Procrastination can be one of the biggest negative traits of an overthinking person, and it would also support your habit of not taking action on time.

Given below are 5 strategies that can help you in ditching the thinking mode and taking action. You can pick any of these as per the situation and break the deadlock. Remember, the longer you remain in the deadlock, the harder it will become for you to get out of it.

The 5 second rule

Fear has a very deep-rooted relationship with postponing things. When you are afraid of doing something, its results, or have a distaste for it, the mind automatically starts overthinking about it. It makes you think about the consequences if things go wrong and would also make you believe that things would go wrong. Many a time, if you don't act on time, the mind will be able to convince you that the time has passed and there is going to be no use of taking the action then.

The mind likes to keep you sitting tied to thoughts. That's the safest playing ground as per the mind.

We only postpone things for the future that we don't like to do. The things for which we don't feel that passionately or the things that have been forced upon us. The things about which we feel passionate, we prepone them. People don't want to get up in the morning even though the alarm clock rings several times and gets snoozed. The reason is their dispassion for getting up. They don't feel excited about the prospects of the day.

The same people would get up hours early if they have to do something about which they are really passionate.

However, you can't be passionate about everything you need to do. Especially not about the things you fear or loath. Yet, inaction will only push you into overthinking.

Make it a rule to get into action within 5 seconds of having the thought. It is a very short window. But you don't need to finish the job in 5 seconds. You simply need to initiate.

For instance, if you need to go to the office, within 5 minutes of the ringing of the alarm clock, you must be off the bed. Any longer you stay there, and your first preference would be to snooze it one last time.

Once you cross the 5 seconds window, your mind would start overthinking the whole process and would surely find things to prove the futility of the whole process.

Get into action before it is too late. This is a great way to break the shackles of procrastination.

Ditching the autopilot

Most of the decisions taken by us are not conscious decisions. They are the decisions taken on instinct. We really don't put much thought into them. This happens because our mind remains on an autopilot mode most of the time.

If you have not been taxing it much about making real decisions, it likes to make decisions based on references. The things you did in similar situations earlier. Did they lead to any negative outcome? What probability of success does it see of for the actions in this attempt?

Your actions are guided by the autopilot in your mind on the basis of such questions. The situations are never judged on their merit. The mind doesn't like to see the probability of the success this time and the conditions that might lead it to the result. It wants to maintain inertia. This is the reason most people procrastinate and never take action. Their mind easily disqualifies most of the possibilities without even considering them a little. The remaining time you'll have at hand now will get utilized for overthinking.

If you want to ditch this trap of overthinking, you must ditch the autopilot. Look at the things mindfully. Take all the decisions consciously. Look at the merit of every situation, and don't try to assume things a lot. This will prepare a better ground for action, and it will also spare you from overthinking when you stop assuming a lot.

Starting positively

One of the biggest reasons for our backing down from taking any kind of action is our tendency to look at things pessimistically. We begin on a negative note and then expect things to end positively. This almost never works.

The negative thought process is disheartening, and it is bad for the initiative. Chiding your own mind will not pump you up; it will push you into inaction.

Try to start anything new, even a day with positive intent. Don't weigh it down with expectations as that may also fill you with worries. Simply set out with a positive note that things would get better from where you start.

If you feel that looking at things in a positive manner from your perspective is not possible due to your limited view, try changing your perspective. Put yourself into the shoes of someone else you could imagine doing a better job at it. Think it through with a different perspective. Sometimes, changing the perspective can bring all the change in the work. The same things that may look very challenging from your angel maybe a piece of cake for others.

Once a man was looking for a famous church in a village. He had come walking from far and was getting grumpy. He saw a boy paying in the way and asked him the distance of the church. The boy thought for a few seconds and said 24,858 miles. The man was awestruck in disbelief. He said that the church couldn't be that far. I have come looking for it from so far.

The boy said that it was 24,858 miles as per the path he had taken; however, it was only 2 miles if he walked in the opposite direction.

Sometimes we simply look at things from a very difficult angle. Looking at it through someone else's perspective can change the whole story.

It can make the work easy and interesting. If you feel stuck at some work and feel that you don't have a going there, try thinking differently from the angle of someone else.

Acknowledging the fears

Fears can push us into inaction. It has a very strong impact on our decision-making skills. If we don't address our fears, it will keep cornering us. Even if we keep avoiding the fears, our mind doesn't sit silently; it makes you think all the time only about those fears and consequences of the actions.

There is no escape from this cycle. If you want to avoid it, the only effective way is to acknowledge your fears.

The moment you acknowledge the fears, they lose the deadly impact they have. You are able to clearly understand the kind of impact they'll have. You also get a chance to look beyond the fears and assess the chances of success clearly.

This is a good way to break the deadlock and come out of the habit of procrastination led by fear.

Learning the Art of Setting Milestones

Our mind is constantly looking for the avenues to push us into inactivity. It seeks ways to push you into inaction, as that is the safest approach.

Many people who began working ambitiously at one point end up in failures not because they had put in the poor effort but because their mind was able to convince them of the futility of their actions.

For instance, you aim to lose 30 pounds and get slim. Your aspirations, external motivations, and inspirations can energize you to begin work in that direction. But it is a task that requires constant motivation as you will be working against your own body. The body would make your work difficult. The mind would assist the body in it.

This means that after a few days, maintaining that motivation can get very difficult. The task of 30 pounds is not something that you are going to get within a few days or weeks, and hence there is a high probability that you'll surrender.

Many people surrender even before they have begun as their mind starts overthinking about the probabilities of success and find none.

Now, think if you had defined your goal in a more accurate way and broken it down into smaller milestones.

You'll lose 30 pounds in 6 months looks like a much well-defined goal. There is a target timeline so that you can't keep postponing it further. This is your first challenge to procrastination.

However, 6 months is a very long period, and maintaining motivation, even with a defined goal, can be difficult.

You also need milestones to help you in your pursuit.

Milestones help you in staging the results in smaller compartments so that you can track your progress.

You need to lose 30 pounds in 6 months means that you have 24 weeks to lose 30 pounds. It brings us to 1.25 pounds per week.

You will have a weekly target, and that can act as your constant motivator. You will have some weeks in which the weight loss would be slower. The milestones would push you to work harder the following week for making up for the deficit.

There will be weeks when your achievements will be higher, and the milestones will pump up to work harder for achieving the final goal faster.

Setting clear goals, dividing them into smaller milestones, and getting into action immediately can help you in breaking the chains of procrastination and inactivity.

Chapter 5

How to Improve Your Mood, No Matter What Are Your Circumstances?

Manage your mind

Taking control of your thoughts and emotions is an important and necessary tool to manage your mind. In reality, if you're not in control of your mind then it is most certainly going to be in control of you. This effective control leads to healthier, more positive choices and habits that can reduce stress and overcome anxiety and depression. It provides you with a framework and the right tools to keep your thoughts from spiraling out of control.

One of the most important keys to managing your mind is understanding that you have the capacity and ability to change. Too often people remain in the same old routine and rut because they don't believe they're capable or worthy of change. Change is inevitable and being ready and willing to embrace change is where the sound, healthy mind comes into play.

Some other ways to manage your mind more effectively could be by filling it with wholesome and positive information. There are many ways this can be achieved - from reading a good book, listening to motivational audiobooks, or even something as simple as a basic daily exercise routine.

Daily habits to manage your mind

There are a number of ways to help you gain better control of your thoughts daily. According to experts, habits are the result of repetitive learning and can be both good and bad. In an article published in Psychology Today, entitled "The Habit Replacement Loop," Dr. Bernard J. Luskin describes three primary characteristics necessary for forming beneficial habits as follows:

1. Attention
2. Focus
3. Purposeful repetition

Some examples of good habits would include things like meditation, reading, writing and exercise. Each of these habits has been known to help manage an overactive mind. Development begins with the decision to make a change, and committing to see that change through. This means learning to manage your time effectively by setting aside the amount of time necessary for each of these practices and making sure you stick to it. You can begin by allocating 15 to 30 minutes daily, which you can also split throughout the day, or between the morning and night. Here are some examples of how to do this:

Daily meditation

Start your day with five to 10 minutes of meditation. Combined with mindfulness and breathing exercises this will help return your body to its natural balance (homeostasis) and a place of relaxation and acceptance of new ideas. It's emptying your head of unwanted thoughts about your day and replacing them with a clear, focused mind instead.

In an article published in the Harvard Gazette, entitled "Meditation study shows changes associated with awareness, stress," affiliate Harvard University students in conjunction with Massachusetts General Hospital (MGH), discovered that by using this form of meditation over a period of only eight weeks of mindfulness meditation training, physical differences to the brain were observed, such as thickening of the hippocampus (responsible for memory and learning) and other changes appeared to the amygdala, which controls anxiety, fear, and stress. Participants of this study confirmed that they felt as though they were more in control of their emotions and mental state.

Positive affirmations

The concept of positive affirmations has been around for a long time. Napoleon Hill introduced them in 1937 in his best-selling book, Think and Grow Rich. They are a set of positive statements structured to reinforce a positive belief system. Most effective when they can be seen or heard several times a day. Repetition at various times of the day can eliminate any negative thought patterns and replace them with positive affirmations.

Positive affirmations must be realistic and something that resonates with you. They should speak to goals you've set for yourself or ways to overcome limiting belief systems. Commit to writing between 10 to 15 positive affirmations and say them at least three times a day for a month.

- "Mistakes are just stepping stones to success. They are the path I must walk to achieve my goals."

- "Every day, I get one step closer to the life of my dreams."

- "I release all negative thoughts about myself and accept myself as I am."

- "I have the power and ability to control my weight through regular exercise and eating healthy."

- "I deserve to be successful and happy."

These are just a few ideas to get you started. There are affirmations you can create to associate with every aspect of your life and give you the necessary boost. Make each one personal, and believable as they are just meant for you.

Practice gratitude

In an article entitled "Giving Thanks Can Make You Happier," (n.d.), published by Harvard University, confirms that a joint psychology study between the University of California and the University of Miami was conducted on the impact of practicing gratitude. Divided into three groups, participants were asked to write a few brief sentences each week on specifically assigned topics. One group was asked to focus on things they were grateful for; another group had to write about things that annoyed them throughout the week; the final group could write about anything that influenced them within the same time frame.

At the end of this 10-week study, those who had focused on gratitude were more optimistic and felt better about themselves. In addition to this, they were more inclined towards incorporating some form of physical exercise into their daily routine and did not visit physicians as often as the group that was asked to write about those things that annoyed them.

End your day with the same routine, but add another exercise where you mentally run through your day. Keep a small notebook or journal next to your bed and before going to sleep, list five things you're grateful for that happened to you that day. They don't need to be big things, but they need to mean something to you. Try not to be repetitive with what you write down, this will challenge your brain to come up with new ideas, breaking down some of the walls of overthinking.

By practicing each of these daily habits and developing a routine, you'll slowly begin to notice that you're moving your mind away from the way you once were. It will take persistence, perseverance, and effort, but remember that it is possible. Repetitive learning is the key to breaking free from the compelling habits of overthinking. You'll start to shift your focus slowly into the present moment, which is exactly where you want it to be.

Chapter 6
Simple Steps to Remove Negative Influences from Your Life

Negativity is a way that we view the world, which is marked by the thoughts and feelings a person expresses toward reality. Negative thinking comes from within a person. Whenever you think negatively, you will only focus on the bad in life and don't reflect enough positivity. As a result, you will think of the worst possible results of an action or decision. Negative people tend to be skeptical of any advice that is given to them, and they don't trust people because of their past experiences.

Even though a person might adopt a negative mindset, it is not healthy, and it hinders your ability to form meaningful connections with other people. Do you tend to look on the bright side, or do you always find things to gripe and complain about? If you are optimistic, you will see things on the bright side. However, if you are a negative person, you will only see the dark side of every kind of situation.

When a negative person is faced with a challenge or difficulty, he or she will automatically default to a negative prediction of what might happen in a given situation.

Where do you get negative thoughts from?

The negative thoughts that arise in our minds come from many places, including the patterns of belief that we develop over time. Our values may include our money, job, relationships, jobs, and other things. If you want to know where your negative thoughts seem to be coming from, then you should ask yourself some questions.

1. Do you find yourself complaining about everything?

2. Do you blame others before yourself?

3. Do you like to predict a negative outcome in any given situation?

In addition to these basic questions, you also should think about things that contribute to your negative thinking, including criticism of people, feeling victimized by different situations, experiencing depression, and always predicting an emergency. As you think about these ideas, then you realize how quickly negative thoughts can spread like wildfire. Whenever you are in the company of people who always think negatively, you will be prone to thinking that way. The more that you hang out with people who have a pessimistic view on life, the more negative you will become. Therefore, it is crucial to find friends you can be with who can build you up instead of those who constantly tear other people down.

Having negative thoughts in your life

When you have negative thoughts, you experience a severe impact on your overall health. Your pessimistic ideas will make your brain go into survival mode, which will be stressed about all situations that arise. When a person experiences chronic stress, they will feel the effects psychologically. Whether you are aware of it or not, you will see that those negative thoughts will affect your ability to function, and they lead to long-term consequences that can jeopardize your well-being. You may find yourself unable to eat a lot, or you may stress eat in order to deal with the situation. When you lose or gain weight, you are likely dealing with negative thoughts as a result of stress on your body.

Negativity can cause you relational difficulties with family members, colleagues, and other people in your circle. When you choose to stay in the negative areas of your life, other people will follow you, and they will be judgmental and critical of different folks that they might come across. Soon, everything rolls over like a domino, bringing you into a lot of stress and anxiety.

In addition to the relational difficulties, negativity almost inevitably results in depression, and depression affects the health and well-being of people. Furthermore, if you are with people who love to tear others down, you would not want to be with them and would rather prefer to go on your own. It is vital to find people who can be an encouraging presence in your life and give you a better influence.

How to remove negative influences from your life?

Now that we have looked at the causes of negativity, we can look at ways to stop being so negative and start living a life that is joyful and positive.

1. Distance yourself from the negative people in your life.

Think of a person that you know who is always negative. Avoid talking to them. Put some distance between you and them. Do not spend too much time with them because if you do, you might get hurt or experience some hard times. It is better if you stop interacting with them at all.

2. Do not feel bad about cutting ties with people who bring you down.

If you have entered into relationships with negative people, you should cut ties with them as soon as possible. Do not forge a relationship with someone who is always negative. You should find people who will build you up and not tear you down. Prioritize building relationships with this latter type of person.

3. Don't get into an argument with a negative person.

If you engage in an argument with a negative person, you will not win. It will be like a drama from a movie or something, and you don't want to see Mount Vesuvius erupt in front of you. Instead of engaging, you should simply walk away from the situation and come back to the person when they are ready to talk. Give that person some space to get over whatever it is that is ailing them.

4. Surround yourself with positive people.

By surrounding yourself with positive people, you will feel more positive and less gloomy. You will feel good to be around this type of people. You will experience a positive outcome, as well.

5. Replace negative thoughts with positive ones.

It is easy for us to get into negative thought patterns, which cause us stress and anxiety. We have to learn to replace negative thoughts with positive ones. We should not let ourselves get into a whirlwind of negative thoughts. Fill your mind with positive thoughts. Experience the amazing power of positive thinking. It will affect your whole day and make you feel much better as a result. For example, maybe you hate going into work on Mondays, and you dread it like the plague. Instead of dwelling on a potentially negative situation, you can say, "I'm excited about going into work today because I can have my coffee, do my work, and spend time with my favorite colleague." When you can have one positive thought, it will make a great difference in your overall outlook.

6. Stop yourself whenever you see yourself spiraling off into negative territory.

The next thing you should do is to notice when you feel that you are slipping into negative territory. Watch yourself lest you get into the pattern of thinking about the negative things in your life. For instance, you may find yourself getting depressed because you watch the news all the time and see the next disaster happen. After seeing this kind of event, your mind defaults to a pessimistic mindset, and you think that a disastrous situation is looming around the corner.

7. Don't complain.

Whenever you find yourself always complaining about whatever is going wrong, you should stop yourself. Hold the thought and then move on with your life. You should not dwell on the negative and think about all the things that are wrong with your life. The truth of the matter is that complaining will do nothing to benefit your life. It will only bring you down. Complaining pushes you away from the things that you want.

8. Don't gossip with other colleagues at the office.

Many of us gossip with other people. It is a contagious thing, and unfortunately, it affects workplaces and schools. It is not helpful to you or anyone in your life. You should avoid it as much as possible. Gossip can tear down communities, and it can result in distrust and many other things.

9. Do not try to read others' minds.

Many times, we might find ourselves wanting to read other people's minds to know what they genuinely think about us. However, we also expect the worst from their thoughts. It is best to stop thinking that people around you have some kind of bad feelings toward you. This will only bring about more stress and anxiety in your life. Moreover, you should stop thinking negatively. Do not jump into conclusions right away; instead, you should keep calm and relax.

10. Stop watching the news or your facebook account

The news feed is one of the most depressing sources of information in our lives, but we always seem to consume a lot of information this way. We go online on the BBC and learn about the latest attack in Somalia or other things that are going on in the world. Bad news can cause us to worry and have bad feelings toward things, and it affects our health. We would do well if we avoid interacting with media that have particularly disastrous consequences for our mental health. The same could be said for Facebook, which advertises fake news, as well as news stories that make us envious of other people and wanting what they have. These sources of information seem to give us more stress and cause us to worry more. The best piece of advice is simply to avoid hanging out in these places. Stop watching the news and endlessly scrolling through your Facebook newsfeed, which only leads to your own unhappiness and dissatisfaction in life. Better yet, simply get rid of Facebook. Deactivate your account and only use Messenger to communicate with your friends.

Chapter 7
How to Develop Self-Confidence

Many people are not born confident. You might be one of them. Fortunately, this value can be worked in various ways to a degree of perfection. When achieved, confidence shall improve the quality of your life immensely.

Think positively

Reality is what you perceive. If you think you feel confident, then you are. Relive your happier situations. Thinking positively is not tricking or kidding yourself but taking control. Do not allow yourself to live on negative thoughts. Learn to stop yourself upon such realization or find a way of reframing them positively. Do not be hard on yourself. When you think positively, you also tend to be more confident with yourself in multiple ways.

Be grateful

The more you think and really affirm that things are working out for you in ways, the more you assert that you are good at what you do and that you have every backing with you. You have the skill, talent, mindset, your loved ones, and a future to go for. That is all you need to get going, and it means a great deal.

Smile

Smile and you will be happier. Do not wait to be happy to smile. Smile and be happy. Smile and notice your stress levels and blood pressure down. A smile is a wall of immunity against disease and negativity. Smile and look more attractive. Be happy and build your confidence. When it all depends on you and you make it look good, then you have no reason to worry.

Speak yourself up

Tell yourself how authentic you are like and your brilliance is unparalleled because you exist in your own right. You owe nothing to anyone. Speak to yourself in the mirror and urge yourself to go out for what you must get, everything and everybody notwithstanding. Speak strength, speak speed, speak accuracy and precision, and speak outcomes because you deserve no less than you want in values, actions, and returns.

Dress intently

When you think you look good for the event, you are more confident about it and yourself. Take the shower, wear clean and on purpose, do the deodorant and just feel collected and put together. Modesty is good but the intent is great and powerful. It is a language encoded and decoded with a pleasure and measure of precision.

Mind your posture

Keep your chin up, your shoulders back, and walk like you own the place. Occupy enough space for you. Look unapologetic. Be flexible, relaxed but stable and fearless. Look confident and so be it.

Work out

Work out to look better. Looking better makes you feel better. What's more, working will make you feel more productive, energized, as well as add vigor and dimension in your moves and activity. Working out makes you feel like you contain yourself and are better able to handle what comes your way.

Wear color

In humans, color has something to do with mood. When you look just bright, it is likely that is how you expect things to go. If you wear a dull color, well that's the kind of reception you anticipate too. The little spike in pizzazz could be all your confidence needs. You may be advised by your friend or stylist early about what colors and garment details to go for during specific events.

Speak with everyone and compliment where due

Contrarian, you may think. When you understand people, you will know how to carry yourself assuredly around them. Simply, do talk to everyone even for a few seconds. People are friendly and will not try to catch or judge you by your statements. Rather the benefits are mutual.

People like being approached for conversation and appreciate it when you break the ice for them. And that is a plus for you.

Chapter 8
Develop the Habits of Successful People

The life you live today is contributed by the habits you have. Habits results to all the success you have achieved. For example, your health, moods, and achievements have been successful because of habits. The activities you take part in shape your life. If, for instance, you engage in bad habits continuously, the bad habits will destroy your life. If you decide to implement good habits, this can change your life forever. It depends on one if he chooses to change his life, then he will make the changes unbeneficial behaviors and replace them with what will benefit him in terms of behaviors. Don't despise the small changes that may take part because they make a great difference in the life of somebody.

Establishing good habits and behaviors takes time to implement; it is not something that will happen in seconds. There methods that can help you to implement the desired behaviors. The following method can be used to help one build new habits:

Setting a trigger

This is having intentions to change the habits and increasing the likelihood of forming a new habit and implementing it. For instance, if you are used to eating chocolates daily, then you can change that habit by saying this to yourself, that when you feel like eating chocolate, then eat the vegetable snack first then chocolate later. You will be building your habits by replacing the bad ones with the good habit. For the new habits to survive, you will need repetition so that they can stick to your mind. Below is the list of the good habits that can be picked by individuals and if they implement them, then they will transform their habits and life completely.

Waking up early

Waking up early will increase productivity because it contributes greatly to the accomplishment of the goals but also brings balance in their lives. You will only get up early if you had enough sleep. This can be achieved if you get to bed early or at a reasonable time and wake up early. You will enjoy life and see the benefits of greater concentrations. You will concentrate if you had enough sleep.

Be ready to learn

Be that person who will be curious to know something, and above all, will be willing to learn that particular thing. If this will continue, then you are going to be a great person sooner than later. Developing the habit of exploring new habits and strengthening existing knowledge can bring a great improvement in your life. What it takes to accomplish all this is the urge to be ready to learn, and you will be boosting your learning curve. Doing this will not take much of your time if you will be more than willing.

Setting priorities

You have several tasks, and you are trying to tackle them at the same time, will you succeed in handling all the tasks? The answer is no, and you need to prioritize the responsibility. Try to see which one has to be done with urgency. It is also good to prioritize your leisure activities and your goals. For example, watching television is of lesser priority than accomplishing tasks that will contribute to your goal. Don't prioritize things that don't contribute to your goals. If they don't add value to your life and goal, exclude them in your priorities.

Have resilience

This will be of great help if stricken by disaster, you easily step up and try to reorganize things before you lose everything. You will have built your mind in a way that it will cope easily and find a solution to the problem you will be encountering. The only way to strengthen resilience is by believing in your abilities. When faced with tribulations, don't give up, but you should keep moving. Move out of a problem by re-organizing things one by one.

Motivating yourself

If you have the habit of motivating yourself whenever you accomplish anything, then forever, that habit will be part of you. This habit will be instilled by yourself. No one else can ignite such a habit in your own life. People may try and motivate you, but with time, you will find that they got tired on the way. You can look for effective ways to do motivation. Keep practicing it each day so that you will keep the fire burning.

Be positive

The way to think can either build you or destroy your life. if you are that person who will always think of failure, then it will happen. You will find that in everything that you try doing then failure becomes part of instead of success. Having positive thinking will act as fuel to your problem. No matter how hard it can be to find a solution to your problem but the positivity you will easily find a solution to the challenge. Being positive has an impact on your life and health. It will help one to live a life with no stress at all.

Have a vision

Are you that person who sees himself or herself succeeding in one way or the other? If you visualize yourself, then it can give positive results. By having a positive vision, then the brain will help you to look into steps in which you will take so that you can accomplish. The main reason why visualization is important is that the mind will be used, and it is hard for the mind to differentiate reality from what it has set to accomplish.

Setting goals

Do you have goals in life? a life without a goal is like going hiking without a map. You will be wandering in the forest, but you will not have the right route out of the forest. Same case in life, no set goals, then no direction in life. You will be wandering doing other things but, in the end, it will not add value to your life. a goal gives you direction, gives the necessary focus to overcome the necessary obstacles in life.

You can do this by writing your goals down, then make it a habit of rereading them daily.

Have room for improvement

It gets to some point in life when you get to abandon the old way and get to create some room for something new. The rule does not only limit us to the old ways but something that will bring a difference to our achievements. It got to bring positive achievement. By doing that, you are creating room for improvement and letting go of things that don't add value.

Make and meet the decisions

The decisions you make can either build or destroy. Be careful when it comes to deciding because the moment they are made, no reverse gear. If planning to change the decision, it may cost you a lot of things. Your success depends greatly on the decision you make. To some other individuals, they spend more time overthinking a problem. By doing that, they will be wasting time on one problem. People don't want to make the wrong decision; that is the reason they will take long before making one. They don't know that deciding whether right or wrong is much better than not making one. Instead of wasting time and you are there, marking your plan and remarking. Act upon what you have at that particular time and will only make adjustments as you move instead of letting indecision to kill your productivity.

Meditation

If you want to change many aspects of your life, then you should start meditating on what you are planning to change. This habit has not been valued by many, and the reason are they see it as a useless habit that cannot help one. In the real sense, this is the habit in which it relieves stress and at the same time, will reduce depression. Those who fear to think, then this can be the best habit for them.

Do physical exercise

When you have regular activities, then you are on the right track of living a healthy life. Regular exercise improves your mental health. By doing regular exercises, then you will be boosting your energy and your mood as well. Once you have, it has a habit, and then you will never be tempted to push it to the next day.

Have little Breaks in life

We have become so busy with life, and we forget to enjoy the little breaks that we get. Nowadays we spend more time on social media forgetting that is depriving us of the times having leisure time. We have many distracters, but if we can slot in time for taking a break, then it will become a habit. At your break, lean back, relax and don't do anything that should take a couple of minutes. The little breaks are effective because, after the break, you will feel refreshed.

Make new friends

When it becomes a habit of meeting someone new every day, it can refresh your mind. You will end up having a different discussion from what you had the preceding day. The different people you will meet will challenge you in different ways. From that, you will be built in all aspects. What is important of all is that you get to meet the right kind of people who will share their private lives stories and professional stories as well. Such people can be a blessing to you.

Learn from those who have made it

When you meet up with new people, you will be able to learn new things from them. It may be hard to meet with those who are experts in a particular field. But you will find that some have written books, others have blog or documentations. Knowing the lives of these experts will act as inspiration on your side. You get to know how they achieved in life, and this will motivate you to do more than what they accomplished.

Listening to others

It is great when people pay attention when you are talking, it is a sign of respect, and it means that you are following what you are saying. But nowadays, what has happened to our conversations? We have people who like to dominate in a conversation. At that particular time, you will find that those who were listening are now thinking about how they will get that chance to also conveyor say whatever idea they may be having. We should be ready to listen to others because by doing that, we will be improving the relationship. It also helps us to be a better negotiator.

In conclusion, it can be hard to have new habits.

You will have many challenges in that journey as you try and getting new habits. At some point in life, you will find that old habits will keep appearing. That should not be the reason for giving up because of the challenges. You should be patient and stick to the new behavior you have acquired for a longer time. After that, you will cross the line, and the new habit will be part of you, and you will engage in it automatically.

Chapter 9
Why and How to Stop Procrastination In Your Life

When talking about procrastination, everyone might relate to it because there isn't anyone who could deny it. At least, once or twice in your life, procrastination would have played its role. Whenever you miss your deadlines, the level of anxiety rises above your head and you are forced to complete the project as soon as possible. But deep down, you know it is impossible to complete because there is so much to do. Yet, you try! Procrastination will make your life miserable, so try not to make it a habit.

Some people want to stop procrastinating, but they are unable to because they don't know how to do it. Or sometimes, they might be missing the motivation they need. And it can be frustrating, I know. You must understand the fact that procrastinating factors differ from one individual to another:

The following are practices that will help you beat procrastination even if you are feeling lazy or unmotivated:

Find solutions to potential emergencies

Procrastination is not just simply a bad habit; rather it is a dangerous one. It will have a huge impact on your health. Sometimes, you might even lose the great bonds that you shared with your family members. They might even come to a point where they assume that you no longer care. There will be situations in life where you have to deal with unexpected priorities such as death, sickness, and much more. Such situations can't wait because you will have to address them immediately. In such an instance, you would have to drop all the scheduled tasks. Some other times, great family events might turn into dreadful situations, and you can't avoid them and get back to your work. Emergencies don't come with a warning, so you have to put up with the obstacles they create. How can you avoid emergencies? Are you going to stop everything and address the issue? Or if you have already delayed the work and then, something urgent comes up, how are you planning to handle it? What might happen when you ignore the emergencies?

To handle emergencies, you have to have a clear picture of the type of emergencies that you are dealing with. You can think about the aftereffects of avoiding the emergency. Or think about the people who are related to the emergency, how will they feel if you ignore it? What are the actions that you can take to solve this sudden issue so that you can get back to work? Or can you put off the emergency issue because it is not life-threatening?

Before you dig in further, let me tell you. If you are working so hard that you don't even have time for your family, it means you are losing a lot of good things in life, there is a lack of balance. You are not living your life — this where the concept of smart working comes into the picture.

Carry out daily evaluations

Another excellent way to avoid procrastination is through daily evaluates. If you allocate ten minutes from your day, you can assess how things are going. When you are doing the evaluate, you will be able to find the priorities of your day. Then, you can analyze the tasks that will have a huge impact on your short-term goals. To make this evaluate session simpler, consider carrying out a Q&A format. What are the scheduled meetings that you need to attend? Are there any emails that you must reply to today? Are there any documents that need to be edited today? Are there any appointments that will take more time than you allocated? What are the tasks that require more attention?

Likewise, you should do a Q&A to find out the layout of the day. But you don't have to stick to the questions that I have mentioned. Instead, you can prepare your own Q&A and follow it. If you do this daily evaluate, you will be able to understand the layout for the day. When you have your layout, you will be able to stay on the track. You will have proper knowledge of the tasks that need more time or a quick response. Hence, you will not procrastinate because you are aware that it will impact your goals negatively.

MIT's or the most important tasks

It's tough to beat procrastination if you begin your day with a to-do-list that bursts with tasks. You must have a simplified to-do-list if you want to get things done on time and correctly. How can you simplify your to-do-list? It is pretty simple if you focus on MIT's - most important tasks. You have to settle for the tasks that will have a considerable impact on your long-term goals. This is recommended by many experts who focus on productivity.

My tips are to select the top three important tasks that need to be handled by the end of the day. It is better to pick two important tasks that have tight deadlines and another that will impact your long-term career goal. If you keep an eye on MIT's concept, you will be able to curb procrastination. Once you complete the two most important activities, you will be interested in doing the other activities by the end of the day. And that motivation is very much needed if you want to succeed in beating procrastination.

The Eisenhower matrix

If you want to make a quick decision, you need the support from the Eisenhower Matrix. The founder of this concept, Dwight Davis Eisenhower, was a general in the army. It was the reason why he invented this concept. It's not always possible to work according to the plan when you are in an army. There will be sudden and important changes. In such an instance, the Eisenhower Matrix concept was the guideline.

If Eisenhower utilized this in the army, there is no reason why we can't utilize this in our lives to avoid procrastination! When you are dealing with this concept, you shouldn't forget the four quadrants related to it. By focusing on the four quadrants, you will be able to approach your day-to-day tasks accordingly. Let me mention the four quadrants in detail:

Quadrant 1: Urgent plus important

These are the tasks that need to be completed first because they are way more important than any other tasks and they directly deal with your career goals. Plus, you must complete the tasks right away because they are urgent. If you complete these tasks, you will be able to avoid negative consequences. Once you get your Q1 tasks completed, you will be able to focus on other tasks. For example, if you have to submit a project by the end of the day, your complete attention should be given to that project because it is both urgent and important.

Quadrant 2: Important yet not urgent

The tasks under Q2 are important, but they are not urgent. Even though they might have a huge impact, they are not as time-sensitive as Q1. Compare Q2 to Q1, and then, you will understand the difference clearly. Typically, Q2 tasks will include the ones that have a huge impact on your long-term career or life goals. Yes, you need to allocate more time and attention to these tasks. But you seldom do it because your mind knows that the tasks in Q2 can wait.

Quadrant 3: Urgent yet not important

The tasks under Q3 are urgent, but you don't necessarily have to spend your time on them. You can either automate or delegate tasks to someone who can handle the work. These tasks are not so important, so it is okay to delegate them. These tasks often come from a third party and the tasks under Q3 will not have a direct influence on your career goals. But when you are handling Q3 tasks, you must note down the tasks that you delegate. For example, if you are working on a time-sensitive project and the phone rings, you might get distracted answering it. Or sometimes, it might not even be an important call. For such activities, you can assign someone. Even if it's an urgent call, you can still assign it to a person who can handle it. Through this, you will be able to manage your day!

Quadrant 4: Not important plus not urgent

The tasks under Q4 include the tasks that need to be avoided. These tasks waste your time unnecessarily. If you don't spend ANY time on Q4 tasks, you will be able to spend more time on the tasks under Q2. By now, you'll know what Q4 tasks consist of. Anyway, they are activities like watching TV, surfing the Internet, playing games, and much more. So, should you eliminate Q4? Well, no! You shouldn't. If you don't have a balanced lifestyle, you might even struggle to protect your job. The tasks in Q4 will help you whenever you take a 5-minute break or whenever you want to step away from work. These tasks shouldn't even be in your mind when you are trying to be productive.

To apply the Eisenhower Matrix to your life, start by drawing a table on a piece of paper or your journal. Then, divide the table into four columns and seven rows. Divide the rows according to the days and add the quadrants to the columns. When your table is ready, analyze your week. But don't write anything down yet. Before you start the day, think, analyze again and allocate the tasks as per the matrix. If something else comes up, you must take some time to analyze the nature of the task, and then classify it in the right quadrant.

5. Do it quickly

Sometimes you come across tasks that don't need a lot of time, not even five minutes, yet you delay it. For example, cleaning after having dinner, sending an email, or even changing into your PJs (this is laziness). Even though these tasks don't take much time, you don't do them because you consider yourself too busy.

Your way of ignoring quick or minor tasks is by telling yourself you have too much to do. But the problem is whenever you delay minor tasks, it builds up into a pile, and you might have to deal with huge tasks at the end. If you don't act immediately, you will have a lot to do when you take days off. Also, if you complete the minor tasks quickly, you will be able to avoid them from accumulating into bigger tasks. There are two practices that you should consider if you want to get minor tasks done.

The Two-Minute Rule is one of the practices that you must follow. If you think that the task will only take two minutes or less, you can do it instead of putting it off, can't you? So, whenever you come across any minor tasks, think whether it will take longer to finish those. If they don't, why not get them done? Also, if you follow this habit throughout, you will feel that you are removing a lot of negativity and you have more time to spend on important tasks. Besides, you'll feel that you are more organized and then you have achieved more than before.

Chapter 10

Ways to Avoid Decision Fatigue

On an average, we make 35,000 conscious or unconscious decisions every day. Most decisions do not need your active involvement. However, even some simple decisions can cost you a lot of time and cause stress. A quick glance at an online sale can cost you an hour. Making the choice of breakfast can be tough for some people. To sleep or to go for a walk can be a harassing dilemma. These decisions can cause decision fatigue. They can make you feel exhausted, spent, or apathetic.

The best way to avoid facing decision fatigue is to follow some simple steps:

Build habits into your schedule

Bringing habits into your schedule is the best way to avoid such decision-making points. If you have a fixed schedule that you follow, then such worries wouldn't arise. Fix a time for daily activities. Following a schedule keeps you sharp and makes you more efficient. It also eliminates the chances of procrastination from your life.

Be firm

The dilemma of whether you are choosing the best or not can be crunching. However, most of the time it is a baseless debate. If there is a product, it is made for the consumption of someone. Do not look for the best qualities in the products, look for the qualities that you desire and once you find them, stick to your decision. Indecisive people radiate a lot of negativity.

Make joy and happiness the parameter for your decisions

The final deciding parameter of most of the things should be the amount of joy it would bring in life. We all have this as the end goal behind all our decisions. However, mostly this is hidden behind riders. If I buy a bigger TV than John, I would have an edge and that would make me happy. This is a bad decision process. John can buy an even bigger TV at any point and then my same TV would start making me feel miserable. If you are going to buy a TV, then the only correct question is the kind of TV that would make you really happy. The kind of viewing experience you would want. The amount of clarity you are looking for. The size that would fit your wall and suit your room size.

Your joy and happiness should be directly behind your decisions and not some hidden agenda. It would take away the decision fatigue.

Choose a role model

Following a role model is always easy when you are picking such habits. It makes your choices simple. If you have a role model then put them in your place for easy and stress-free decision making. Imitating their decisions will absolve you of all the responsibility and fatigue. The ultimate goal of the practice is to ensure that you have to make a fewer number of such decisions on a daily basis.

You do not have to lose your identity. It is only for taking decisions that have no effect on the course of your life. In fact, easy decision-making process frees up a lot of time for you. You will be in a better position to ponder over the larger problems in a relaxed manner.

Learn to say 'No'

Being resolute is very important for the success of any such exercise. Despite your efforts, there will be times when you'll be standing at the crossroads. You'll have to learn to firmly make a decision and go with it. You may not have the clarity but if you keep fighting with the idea, it will lead to stress. Learn to live by your decisions.

Some simple stress saving habits

Eating similar food

Food is an important choice that we make every day. You have several meals a day. If you start spending 10-15 minutes before every meal to decide the menu, you are doing a great disservice to yourself and humanity. You are only useful for the food-producing industry. The best way to expedite the process, or to make it simple is to either plan in advance for the week or month or eat similar food daily. You can have minute variations but stick to the same script. This will save a lot of time and effort.

Have a smaller wardrobe

Trim your wardrobe as much as possible. The lower the number of choices in clothes you have, the shorter you'll take to get ready. It will save time and you wouldn't have to ponder about your shining armor daily. Limited choice of clothes is a strategy adopted by some of the most successful people in the world.

Follow daily routines

Follow daily routines like a clockwork. If you are being lenient about your routines then you are cheating yourself. Stick to the routines as they help in the formation of rigid habits. Look at the people retiring from military service. They need to train daily in the morning for around two decades. It is a compulsion in the beginning. But they find it hard to shun the habit even after they have retired. The routine becomes a part of their life. It keeps them fit and functioning.

Have fixed corners in your schedule

Do not compromise with the time of separate activities. Everything has a definite importance in life. If you have designated a specific time of the day to one activity, do not try to fit the other into it. This adjustment trains your mind to make a compromise. It also has to make an unnecessary decision. Strictly avoid it in all circumstances.

If something makes you feel anxious, drop it

Do not do things that cause stress. Modern life mandates us to do several things in peer pressure. This is tiring and uninspiring. If you do not like anything, learn to stay away from it. It will cause unnecessary levels of stress and anxiety which you had been trying to avoid in the first place.

Do not fall in the trap of problem of choice

Economists say that the biggest problem of this world is not poverty or hunger; it is the problem of choice. Rich or poor, man or woman, healthy or sick, we all have to face this problem. We have to make numerous decisions on a daily basis. Some decisions make you feel liberated and others crush you down. The marketing industry has perfected the art of using the problem of choice to its advantage. They put you in the trap of choosing between better and worse, small and big, cheap and costly, bright or dull, light or heavy and in the process, you end up making choices that were not even required. Keep your choices simple if you want to remain happy and stress-free for the whole of your life.

Chapter 11
Challenging Your Thoughts

To stop overthinking, you need to first retrain your brain. Fortunately, there are many exercises and activities that you can use to reshape the way you think.

Now that you know a little about overthinking, and you also know when you are on the verge of dropping into that deep whirlpool of infinite negative emotions, you can start getting rid of it entirely, and you can start by challenging your thoughts before they run out of control.

Before you begin

Here are some of the things that you need to know before you start challenging your negative thoughts so you will not get too surprised and overwhelmed with everything that is happening.

1.   You need to know that challenging your thoughts might feel unnatural, sometimes even forced at first. But with a bit of practice, it will start to feel natural and believable.

2.   To build up your confidence for thought challenging, you should practice them on thoughts that are not as upsetting and provides a bit more flexibility. It is also a good idea to practice this technique when you are still feeling a bit neutral and not too overwhelmed by your

thoughts. Trying to practice thought challenging after a particularly rough and problematic day would be asking too much from yourself.

3. The first couple of times you try thought challenging it would be best if you jot down your responses. Often, when beginners try doing it in their heads, they end up with their thoughts going around in circles, which makes their thoughts all the more intense, and might cause them to spiral into overthinking.

4. Another benefit of taking down notes is that if a similar thought pops up in the future, you can refer to your notes and find out how you reacted to it.

5. You can practice with a family member or a friend whom you know will not judge you. Practicing with another person might help you by shedding light on the blind spots of your thinking, or they can offer you different viewpoints that you might find useful.

6. When you are first practicing thought challenging, you should focus on a single thought instead of a series of them this early in the game. For instance, instead of thinking "It's pretty obvious that my bosses thought I messed up the project" you should break down your thoughts into smaller, simpler sentences, and then challenge these thoughts one by one. You will only be confusing yourself if you start challenging a pile of thoughts at the same time.

7. Do something that will distract yourself once you finish working through a couple of thought challenging questions. This will give you some time for your mind to settle down.

Now that you know what you should expect, here are some of the most popular thought challenging exercise that you can try now.

Step back and assess the situation

Here's a scenario that you might have experienced: you feel as if your boss is constantly and intentionally ignoring you. You think that the reason why your boss did not greet you this morning is because you somehow messed up something and that he is contemplating firing you very soon. Usually, this kind of thought will cause your mind to overthink and cause you to lose sleep, thus causing you to not be as efficient at work, which therefore leads to you getting fired; in short, overthinking problems turns them into self-fulfilling prophecies.

On the other hand, if you just step back and analyze your thoughts before your overactive brain blows it way out of proportion, you can control it better. Next, think about what you could do in order to not get fired, like increasing your productivity, or maybe learn a new skill that can help you do your job better.

In just a couple of minutes, you have derailed your train of negative thought before it even gets a chance to gain momentum.

Write them all down

Another way to challenge your negative thoughts before they trigger you to overthink is to write them all down on a piece of paper. When you write down the things that are bothering you, it gives them a somewhat tangible form, which actually helps you reanalyze them in a more rational manner. If you want to take this to the next level, you can start making a thought journal.

What is a thought journal/diary?

A thought diary is different from the traditional form of journaling, it has a structure that you have to follow to make analyzing your thoughts much easier. For instance, in a thought diary, you do not start an entry with a "Dear Diary" or any form of it, the entries look more like a ledger if anything.

You make a thought diary by making a couple of columns on the page and then you title them as follows:

Antecedent – These are the things that triggered you during the day.

Beliefs – These are your thoughts about the things that you listed in the first column.

Consequences – These are the things that happened because of your thoughts.

This is why a thought journal is called an ABC journal.

Here is an example of how you write an entry in your thought journal. You suddenly start worrying because you have an upcoming bill that you have to pay, this is your consequence. In the second column, you write that you were worried because you might not be able to make your due date.

After some time of writing in your thoughts journal, you might start noticing that the triggers are usually not related to the thoughts that made you worry. Thoughts just occur, and the triggers that caused them to surface might be related to them at all; thoughts are fickle in that way.

In the consequence's column, you then might write down something like, "I took an aspirin to get rid of the headache that I felt was coming."

Every Sunday evening you could evaluate your entries and then think of the things that you could have done better. For instance, for the entry above, instead of taking an aspirin, you could have just walked around the park to clear your mind, or at the very least you could have eaten an apple or something just so your headache will not get any worse. Or you could call your utility company and inform them that you might be a little late on the payment, but you will be paying, and ask if it is possible for them to waive the late fees. Your thought diary will help you make sense of your muddled thoughts by laying them out on paper for you to easily analyze. This tool can help you understand your less-than-ideal coping skills and why you end up making choices that lead to consequences that are not really best for you. With the help of a thought journal you can change your future consequences by restating and reanalyzing your past thoughts and making the necessary adjustments.

Benefits of a thought diary

Writing in a thought journal/diary helps you identify the things that trigger you into overthinking. When you write down your thoughts, you will easily see if they are actually legitimate concerns, or if they are just irrational. Thought journals help you recall how you behaved during the time you were triggered into overthinking, and in time you will start to notice the patterns in the way you think.

When you recognize your existing thought patterns, it will be possible for you to change not only your behavior but also your thoughts. When you notice evil thoughts start to creep in, you can practice mindfulness and just observe and acknowledge them so they will go away. You actually do not need to behave according to your thoughts, you can actually ignore them and just continue living your own life. It is much better to write down "I ignored the thought of..." instead of "I went to the pub and drank a few pints to make myself forget," and if you notice that you are doing basically the same thing almost every day then your thought diary is actually working.

Make a habit of writing a thought journal

You can use a small notebook, a stack of papers, anything that you can write on and keep confidential. No one else aside from you and your therapist (if you are seeing one) must know about the existence of this journal; no one else should have access to your inner thoughts.

If you do not want to use the traditional method, you can also use your smartphone or laptop to create a secret document. Gradually over time, you will start noticing when you are starting to spiral into overthinking and then stop yourself from going any further.

Negative emotions, like those that shatter your confidence to pieces, can usually lead to clinical depression, which makes you feel irrationally lonely, hopeless, and they will break you apart from the inside. Writing helps you get rid of your self-destructive thoughts. It is an art that can help you share your innermost feelings and your deepest thoughts.

Writing down your feelings onto paper is a way for you to freely express your views and opinions on the things that happened during the day, and what effect they had on your life. You are not just writing words on paper, you are effectively eliminating all these negative thoughts from your mind, and with them goes all that negativity that came with them.

Get a hobby

Have you always wanted to learn to play the piano, the guitar, ukulele, or any other kind of musical instrument, why not try learning today? Do you want to get good at drawing, calligraphy, or painting? Attend classes or watch online video tutorials. You can also play your favorite video games for an hour or so. Having a hobby not only gives you a creative outlet, but they also provide you with a way to create something with your hands, it also allows you to think individually, and most importantly, hobbies provide you with an escape from your negative thoughts.

Whenever you feel as if your thoughts are starting to overwhelming you, whip out your hobby kit, and immerse yourself in the activity. Lose yourself in the skills, coordination, concentration, and repetition that your hobby requires you to do. Focus your mind on the comfort or challenge brought about by your chosen hobby, and allow it to chase away all of the worries that used to trigger your overthinking.

Chapter 12
Mental Clutter

What is mental clutter?

What comes into your mind when you hear of mental clutter? Do you visualize a physical clutter that you know of? Mental clutter simply means mental overload, mental stress or mental fatigue. This is anything that gives you anxiety, depression, frustration, sense of overwhelm, and anger. This clutter comes in the form of:

- Regrets for past failures and regret for not doing some things that you should have done

- Too many bills to pay and increasing debts as well as unfinished projects

- Worries and insecurities

- Inner critic

- Feeling bad for failing to achieve something

What causes mental clutter?

Worry

When we encounter challenges in our daily activities, our brains naturally go to a state of worry. Although it is a natural reaction, we can always control it because it will not solve any of our problems. Instead, worrying will worsen the situation. Worrying will take away your peace of mind and it will stress you. Worrying is a waste of energy.

The best thing you can do is to stop worrying. Find something to do that will divert your thoughts to something better like going for a walk, dancing, cooking or anything that interests you. You can also write down those things that are robbing you of your peace of mind and write how you are going to solve them.

Regret

Gee whiz! "I wish I worked hard in school my life could be better!" Such remarks are common when having a conversation with friends or family members. We all have those things we wish we had done or not done in our lives! Sometimes our minds can focus on those things but we should not allow it. Focusing your minds on regrets will rob you of your happiness and cause you mental fatigue and stress. You cannot change the past so put your energy into creating a better vision for your life.

Fear

Fear is an enemy of progress! You should not allow fear to hinder you from taking chances and chasing after your dreams and enjoying life.

Do you dream of owning a business but you are afraid that it might not take off if you start? Start it anyway and silence the fear that you have.

Guilt and shame

We should take responsibility for our wrongdoings and learn some lessons from it. Never allow yourself to be a prisoner of guilt and shame because it will cause you to have resentment self-hate, and even kill your self-esteem. The best way to get rid of guilt and shame is to acknowledge your mistake, forgive yourself and move on. This will empower you, motivate you to become a better person, make you value yourself. You should never repeat the same mistake.

The inner critic

How do you perceive yourself? Do you frequently have negative self-talk dominating your mind? Negative self-talk will limit our mental growth and lower our self-confidence. Remember your brain will believe what you tell it. If you constantly tell yourself that you cannot do it, your brain will act according to that belief.

You need to learn to refuse negative self-talk and replace it with positive talk. If the inner critic is telling you that you cannot do it then do it and you will silence that inner critic that is hindering your progress in life. Talk to yourself positively every day and you will see changes and your self-confidence and esteem will improve making you feel good about yourself.

14 Tips to clear mental clutter

Mental clutter can greatly lower your productivity because you will lose focus and concentration. Assess your life, identify the source of your mental clutter, and try to fix it. Remember, the design of the brain does not allow it to divide its attention in too many directions. That is the reason why it needs to be orderly and peaceful so that it can filter information into the right place and act.

To get your mind in a good state, you need to clear it of any clutter. You should organize your thoughts, worries, and tasks so that your mind can have somewhere for focusing and acting accordingly. The following are some of the tips that can help you to get rid of mental clutter.

Declutter your physical environment

When you sit in an environment that is full of clutter, it will cause your mental clutter. This is because the clutter will keep on telling your mind that it needs to work extra hard to clear the clutter. These excessive stimuli will likely suck your mental energy. If you clear the clutter from your physical environment, you will also be clearing your mind from the mental clutter.

Get rid of the non-essential items and put everything else in its rightful place. The best way to clear your mental clutter is by clearing your environment or workspace every day so that clutter does not pile up. Tidying up your workspace will promote your mental clarity.

Write a "to-do" list

You do not have to overwork your brain by storing so much information in it. Having a "to-do" list where you write all that you have to do will free up your mind. The list should have priorities of tasks and you should check them daily and work on them depending on their priorities on the list. The list can have appointments, projects, bills to pay and so on. You can always tick against a task when you complete it.

This list can help you in collecting your scattered thoughts and tasks. Work on the critical tasks first then you can move to the less critical tasks.

Keep a journal

A journal is almost similar to a "to-do" list, but here you document those things that disturb your peace of mind and give you anxieties and worries. You can write down your worries, plans for achieving certain goals, and even problems in your relationship that are draining your peace of mind.

Commit to remain in the present

You need to let go of your past. Holding on to regrets from past mistakes or missed opportunities, or people who have hurt you, will clutter your mind and rob you of your mental peace. Getting rid of unnecessary thoughts and fears will reduce stress and improve your confidence. These negative memories do not help you at all, so try to delete them in your mind so that you can have a better focus on the things that are more important in your life.

Avoid multitasking

Organize your work well and tackle them on a priority basis. This will prevent you from straining and you will reduce stress and overwhelm. Although multitasking may seem like being counterproductive, it will eventually limit your concentration span and stress you. If you find your home or office is in a mess, start by clearing the clutter before handling any other business. Clear your mind of any other thoughts and focus on clearing the clutter.

Limit the amount of information you consume

The amount of information that we consume can have an impact on our mental health. Too much information from the media, newspapers and the internet can clog our brain causing stress and anxiety. Spending so many hours reading some information on social media, blogs or any other platform can clutter our minds with unnecessary stuff causing mental fatigue and mental stress.

You should limit the amount of time on social media and select only important information to read. You should never allow yourself to consume negative content and cancel any blog subscription that does not help improve your life. Ensure that the information you read is authentic and from a credible source, then store only relevant information while you discard the rest.

Set priorities

What are your goals in life? You should identify which things are most important in your life and which ones are not. Setting priorities can help you in taking control of your life and it can help you in identifying and reaching your goals in life. Having an endless "to-do" list can clutter your mind. You should know that you could not do everything in one go. So, decongest your mind by having a top priorities list.

You can start by writing down a list of what you want to do and achieve based on priorities. The next thing is to plan on how you will do the tasks and how you will achieve your goals. After writing down how you are going to execute your plan, you can now allocate each task the time you will take to finish it. Keep checking and updating your priorities to ensure that they remain relevant because they can change over time.

Make decisions on time

Postponing decision making will clutter your mind with pending decisions. So, act right away and avoid procrastination. However, remember to evaluate your decisions first before implementing them. Therefore, if you delay decisions, you are simply cluttering your mind. Check your emails, letters, bills, requests and respond to them accordingly so that they do not pile up giving you mental clutter.

Put your decisions on autopilot

Daily tasks that require decision-making can clutter your mind. Examples of these daily tasks that require daily decision-making include:

- Deciding on what to cook for breakfast, lunch or dinner
- Deciding on what you will wear to work
- Deciding on which TV channel to watch the news

You should prevent your mind from cluttering with these daily tasks for example:

- You can design a weekly schedule for meals indicating which food for each day and meal
- You can watch specific TV channels at specific times
- Set specific clothes that will take you through the week
- Set specific days' tasks like doing the laundry on Saturday

Practice meditation

Meditation is a great way of relaxing your mind and clearing it of any stressful thoughts. You need to make it a daily practice to help you eliminate any unnecessary thoughts and to calm your mind.

Take some time to unwind

Take a break from your busy schedules and stressful situations. Take a walk in the park, go swimming, go to social events, and go for hikes or anything that will calm you and make you happy. Give your mind rest and let it recharge so that you can improve your focus and mental clarity.

Share your thoughts

Sometimes talking to someone eases the emotional burden and clutter in our minds. You can share your thoughts with a trusted friend or a family member. This can help you to see things differently and make sound decisions.

Practice breathing exercises

Taking a deep breath and exhaling slowly can work magic by calming your mind and relaxing your nerves. Deep breathing can also clear your mind giving you a calm mood. It is also helpful in reducing stress and promoting concentration.

Eat healthily and get enough sleep

A good diet and good sleep are essential to your mental health. Getting enough sleep will help your mind to rest and recharge. This is also the best remedy for reducing stress and fighting depression and anxiety.

Chapter 13

Embracing Mindfulness as an Efficient Alternative to Overthinking

Worrying blurs your mind and prevents you from seeing clearly. Instead, embrace mindfulness.

What's mindfulness?

In simple terms, mindfulness is the average ability of a man to be completely conscious of his current location and what he is doing in that location and not being distracted by what goes on within his environment.

Naturally, everyone is blessed with the concept of mindfulness within them; notwithstanding, it can only be accessed when it's consistently used. But how do you know you've become mindful? You become conscious of what is going through your brain. When you consistently teach your mind to be mindful, you redesign your brain.

Further, the aim of mindfulness is to be conscious of their inner operations of the function of the brain, its physical processes, and feelings. If, by chance or knowingly, we lose grip on the critical things in life, life may leave us behind. With mindfulness, we can be more present, more aware, and more capable of dealing with life.

How people define mindfulness

Some have defined mindfulness as a condition of being conscious of one's current situation. They say that individuals who do not judge situations as either good or bad are not being controlled by their thoughts and that these individuals can be tagged as being mindful.

Being mindful is a useful tool to help one understand and control subconscious feelings that may present big problems in both our work and personal relationships. Mindfulness suggests being in the current moment instead of dwelling on the past or peering into an unknown existence. As a tool, mindfulness has been defined by many to be utilized during meditation.

Many see mindfulness as therapeutic. There are a series of advantages to being mindful. Some of these benefits include reducing a person's level of anxiety and depression and boosting a person's general well-being, helping them to combat feelings of isolation and rejection.

The best way to lead a mindful life

A person's emotional condition determines their ability to remain objective in stressful situations. Dwelling on painful memories and past events can haunt people and prevent them from doing their very best within their individual environments.

A man or woman may have, many years ago, doing something wrong, and years after year, the thought will keep returning and haunting him or her. He may want something to happen that will take away the thought of remembering that occasion. But how could that be solved?

This person would need to focus on that reality that is existing within his/her environment, and not let his past regrets disturb his/her present happiness. There is no doubt that the best tool to help a person to be conscious of what happens within his or her environment is mindfulness; it enables us to stop judging whether the situation is good or bad.

If you really want to control your feelings, mindfulness is something you should practice.

Important facts to know about mindfulness

These mindfulness facts are important for you to know. Knowing them will allow you to understand mindfulness and appreciate its functions.

Fact 1: Mindfulness is not a myth or farce.

Developing mindfulness is a scientifically-proven method which will result in improved relationships **with friends, neighbors, families, coworkers, and other individuals.**

Fact 2: You need not alter your personality.

We don't need to change anything about our personality to become capable of being present. Changing who you are will achieve little or no success at all; methods like these are bound to fail. But with mindfulness, you can bring the best out of yourself and become a new, improved you.

Fact 3: Everyone can learn mindfulness.

Mindfulness is gained by learning and practicing. And it is very easy; anyone can learn how to become more mindful.

Fact 4: Mindfulness is a way of life.

Mindfulness is not just common practice; it is a way of life. This way of life helps us to get rid of mindless stress and handle life's challenges more easily.

Fact 5: Evidence supports the benefits of mindfulness.

The effects and benefits of mindfulness have been observed in scientific studies and in the personal experiences of those who practice it. These studies indicate that mindfulness improves health, general well-being, and all other aspects of human lives.

Fact 6: Mindfulness gives birth to innovation.

Mindfulness eliminates mental clutter and frees the mind up for creative and intellectual pursuits. You will find it easier to provide answers to complex situations and problems.

Fact 7: There are some mindfulness practice basics.

With mindfulness, your reaction to daily events becomes more positive. Self-control is improved, making the impact of mindfulness more beautiful.

Wondering how to go about practicing mindfulness? Here are some important steps to follow;

- Set aside time and space for your practice.

For effective mindfulness practice, it is best to schedule a regular time and place. Always set time and space aside for this task.

- Do not pass judgment on your thoughts.

The chances that we will judge our thoughts while practicing mindfulness are high. The right thing to do is to observe such thoughts without passing judgment.

- Have a positive view of the present moment.

The goal of mindfulness is not only to achieve unmatched calmness and quietness; it is actually to increase our attentiveness to each moment, without judging it to be good or bad. Hard as it may be, the goals of mindfulness are achievable.

- Accept each moment as it is.

We might easily get lost in thought. The best way to come back to the present is through mindfulness.

- Stop your mind from wandering mindlessly.

At every moment, numerous thoughts will pop into your head. But never let these thoughts be the basis for your judgment. Identify the point at which your mind starts to wander and refocus it on the present moment.

These following practices will help you achieve mindfulness more easily. They are simple, but you must be dedicated and work hard to bring about positive results.

Mindful practices to help you improve your life

A positive change in attitude and the effectiveness of your activities increase when you can set time aside each week to practice mindfulness or mindful exercise. This exercise will help you to become more patient and better tolerate others. Your mind will worry less about criticism or negative comments. It will result in you socializing more easily and becoming friendly.

The result will definitely affect your sleep. You will get a sound and peaceful night's rest. Overall, your day will be eventful, happy, and you will feel fulfilled long into the evening.

Mindful walking

Think about what you want to do for 15 to 20 minutes each day while walking. This is mindful walking. Since walking helps to keep you refreshed and improve thinking, mindful walking has a definite purpose. To get better results, you have to stick to a particular pattern and method. This will enhance your progress.

You need to be attentive and concentrate well if you are engaging in mindful practices. Endeavor to pay attention to even the littlest of details, such as the people and events around you. Four essential elements will make mindful walking possible: a steady pace, relaxed gaze, straight posture, and good balance.

Posture

The success of mindful walking is influenced by your posture. You need to hit that perfect position while you engage in mindful walking. Getting the right posture involves releasing your body into each moment. Getting rid of stiffness, standing in an upright position, and ensuring that your feet are planted firmly on the ground. This will help you to walk better.

Balance

To avoid distraction while engaging in mindful walking, you need to have the right balance. This balance should be obvious from your finger down to your arms, and even to your tummy.

You may need to do this to be successful; bend the left thumb and wrap the other finger around it. Then place it on your stomach. Now place the right hand on it and let your right thumb rest in-between the left thumb and the index finger.

Gaze

Your gaze level affects your attentiveness to things around you, and how well you concentrate. More success is achieved when you lower your gaze; don't necessarily look at the ground, though. Remove or lower your gaze when you start to become too focused on the things that you see around you.

Pace

During mindful walking, your pace is another thing to consider. Walking too fast will help you achieve nothing. Try a steady pace; walk slowly, or at least below your average walking pace. When your feet touch the ground, it will help you to feel more grounded at the moment and able to concentrate.

Why should you practice mindfulness?

There are many misconceptions about mindfulness. Therefore, people who start engaging in mindfulness often find that the results are very different from what they expect or from what they have been promised.

Below are some of the six most frequent misconceptions about mindfulness:

- The goal of mindfulness is to make you a better person.

- The goal of mindfulness is to halt your ideas.

- Mindfulness is a religious practice.

- Mindfulness will protect you from being affected by real-life conditions.

- Mindfulness will solve all your problems.

- The goal of mindfulness does not go beyond eliminating stress.

Yes! Mindfulness helps people to deal with their stress, but that is not the main objective of mindfulness. What then, is the goal? It is to ensure that you are conscious about what is happening around you: things happening in the physical, mental, and emotional faculties. Start learning mindfulness today for the following reasons:

Train your body to thrive via mindfulness

One thing that has helped athletes to surpass their own expectations, achieve greatness, and rid themselves of negativity is mindfulness. Their training often involves channeling their strength in the best possible way and gaining better control of their breathing.

Athletes can attain full presence and achieve their goals when they work on a mix of mindfulness, which includes tactical breathing, and intellectual, behavioral exercises.

Boosting your creativity via mindfulness

By becoming more mindful, you can clear your mind, freeing yourself up to become more creative in all of your daily tasks or assignments.

Strengthen your neural connection via mindfulness

The development of new neural routes and building new connections in the brain can be made possible through the practice of mindfulness. This improves your abilities and helps you concentrate more on things that are currently happening around you. It also helps you become more flexible and promotes well-being.

Chapter 14
Effects of Overthinking

There is a high possibility of experiencing somatopsychological problems if your vagus nerve is inflamed or damaged. These problems are mostly related to your psychological aspect and can only be noticed through your actions, and they initiated in your head as it depends on how your brain responds to different situations, so you need to understand the two systems of the vagus nerve continuously communicate with the brain, mainly about other body organs. The sympathetic nervous system is responsible for keeping you in action by feeding the cortisol and the adrenaline while the parasympathetic nervous system is reliable while you are relaxed or resting.

In other words, the sympathetic system activates actions while the parasympathetic decelerates actions and keeps you at rest. However, the latter utilizes acetylcholine as neurotransmitters that control the blood pressure and the heart rate to create a perfect condition for relaxation. As a part of the body's autonomous nervous system, the vagus nerve may fail or experience damage hindering its full potential to the body. The most common condition that affects the vagal nerve is inflammation that makes it malfunction. This condition could worsen the functioning of the whole body as the vagal nerve facilitates essential processes that keep the body healthy and kicking. This stage discusses the psychological problems that arise as a result of vagal dysfunction and inflammation as follows:

Chronic stress

The problem is associated with overthinking things that might be beyond your control. Stress can also be a result of issues in your vagal nerve. For instance, when your body is exposed to harmful situations, it releases chemicals that are meant to respond appropriately and avoid injury. As noted, before, the sympathetic nervous system stimulates the response through the fight-or-flight reaction, and it is at this time that your heart rate increases to quickly supply blood to the rushing body parts and muscles. The response likewise enhances the quickened inhalation of oxygen to assist in blood oxygenation. In this case, stress acts as a protective mechanism that your body initiates to keep you alert and out of danger.

There are different perceptions of stress among people. In other words, what causes stress for one person might be of little concern to the other, and people have different ways and potential to deal with it. This means that if stress is meant to prevent you from danger, then it should not be treated as a bad thing. Besides, our bodies have a unique mechanism that is intended to deal with specific doses of stress. However, the body's capabilities could weaken as you may be overwhelmed by chronic stress that could be as a result of vagal nerve inflammation or damage. This type of stress impacts almost every aspect of your life, including physical health and emotions. The chronic stress is also characterized by low esteem where you feel worthless and not comfortable while in public.

If you are suffering from chronic stress, you are likely to feel overwhelmed and easily agitated by others. As a result, you end up avoiding interactions with your peers as you feel they want to control you. Avoiding people and having low self-esteem makes you suffer in isolation as you may not realize the seriousness of the condition. With this in mind, the emotional symptoms of chronic stress could end up being a serious condition if not detected and treated. Consequently, your judgment becomes impaired by the condition as you get prone to the inability to focus and forgetfulness. You also remain pessimistic and unable to view your life positively and exhibit nervousness through behaviors such as fidgeting and nail-biting.

First, people with chronic stress seem to avoid complex responsibilities. They also experience sudden changes in your appetite where they either eat excessively or not eat at all. Second, procrastination is also associated with chronic stress, and you could be at risk of indulging in alcohol and drug abuse. Therefore, you should ask for feedback if you think that you are suffering from stress.

Anxiety and panic attacks

Whenever you come across a stressful situation, the body activates the sympathetic nervous system of the vagus nerve. In most cases, the system is reversed once the situation is over. However, the persistence of the tension would mean that the sensitive effect of the vagus nerve would be prolonged until you are out of harm's way. The effect is usually triggered and ended by a physiological response in your body, but a prolonged fight-or-flight response would cause problems for your body. The situation would lead to the activation of the intestine and the adrenal axis of the brain. As a result, the brain increases the production of hormones that travel through the bloodstream to stimulate the adrenaline and cortisol induction.

The hormones act as inflammatory precursors and immune suppressors, causing the anxiety that could make you ill and depressed, so the chronic anxiety increases the production of glutamate in the brain, which, when combined with cortisol, reduces the hippocampus in charge of memory retention. The worsening of this situation leads to the development of anxiety disorder characterized by panic attacks. The problem is characterized by a sense that you are in an impending danger or your life is at risk. These false signs may be frequent, depending on the seriousness of the condition. With this condition, you feel afraid of losing your valuables or as if you are about to die. In most cases, the effect seems uncontrollable as the panic creates an illusion that it has been decided elsewhere.

At this time, your heart rate is increased due to the tension, making it pound on your chest as your breath goes wild. The blood pressure increases as the body take it as an attack. These panic attacks might confuse your body as they give false alarms making your body sweat as if you are in a serious situation even though you may be lying on your couch. The helplessness associated with anxiety and panic attacks leaves you trembling with fear of imagined imminent danger, and you will realize that your body is shaking uncontrollably due to a perceived situation.

Phobias

Vagal inflammation is known to cause phobias as one of the somatopsychological problems in the human body. Mostly, the problem is characterized by a deep sense of panic and irrational fear reaction. When you are in this condition, you encounter different sources of fear, depending on how you perceive the environment. In some instances, you could be experiencing phobia in specific situations, objects, or places. This form of vagal nerve damage is known to complicate how your brain interprets some aspects of the environment, so you end up feeling insecure in dark or quiet environments, especially if you have had a frightening experience before.

The effects of phobia vary depending on the seriousness as well as the body's mechanism to repair damaged tissues. These conditions determine the impact of phobia in your body as it could only be an annoying experience or build up to a severe and disabling. If you experience phobia, you might be helpless about it as it is caused by other underlying conditions such as vagal nerve inflammation. Therefore, you are prone to stress as you always remain afraid of a possible attack, making you unproductive and unsocial, especially in the workplace. The condition may be different from one person to the other, hence the different categorization according to the trigger and symptoms.

One common type of the condition is known as agoraphobia which is characterized by the panic of situations and places that you cannot escape from. Mostly, people who have an agoraphobia are afraid of being in open places such as outside their houses or in crowded places. People feel uncomfortable while in social areas and like to stay most of their time indoors. The main reason why these people avoid public places is due to the anxiety of experiencing phobia publicly, which might embarrass them and leave them helpless. In some cases, people with an agoraphobia may experience a health emergency, making them remain in places where they could ask for an urgent response.

Social phobia has relatively similar characteristics and is also known as social anxiety disorder when combined with symptoms of anxiety. As the name suggests, the victims of this disorder avoid social places and prefer staying in isolation for fear of humiliation and discrimination in case they become phobic. This type of phobia is as serious as it could be caused by a simple interaction such as answering a phone call or talking to a stranger. It makes the victims go out of their way to avoid these interactions making life hard for them, especially if they are working or attending school. A phobia may be triggered by a specific object with common categories being the environment, medical, situations, or animals.

Bipolar disorder

The problem is also caused by vagal dysfunction and inflammation and was formerly referred to as a manic depression. It is a mental condition that triggers a moody feeling and swinging emotions. When the emotions are high, they are referred to as mania or hypomania, and depression when they are low. If you are depressed, you probably will experience hopelessness, sadness, and lost pleasure and interest. The feeling makes you hate activities that you liked before and lose interest in meeting the people you love. However, the feeling is sometimes short-lived as you may suddenly experience high moods that make you feel euphoric and irritably full of energy.

The drastic changes in mood significantly affect how you behave, judge, or sleep. It also hinders you from clear reasoning and making the right decision. There are numerous episodes of these mood swings that occur several times annually. In some cases, you may experience changes in events and emotional symptoms, while others may not experience them at all. The condition is manageable through the follow up of a treatment plan that includes counseling and medication. When a dysfunctional vagus nerve causes the condition, it could only be treated by healing the nerve. Several types of this disorder include depression and hypomania. These symptoms could cause drastic life effects and significant distress if left unaddressed.

Bipolar disorder is experienced when the condition triggers a break from reality and makes you fear your imagination. It is characterized by a single manic episode and occurs either before or after the incident. Bipolar II is characterized by a major depressive episode that lasts for weeks followed by a hypomanic episode that happens for about a week. The condition is more common in women but is also experienced by men. In cyclothymia, you experience bouts of depression and hypomania, which are relatively shorter than those caused by the last two types. Additionally, the condition is characterized by a month or two for stability when the problem recurs and extends for some weeks. The mania and hypomania episodes are distinct in their symptoms, but the mania episode is more severe and is known to cause problems in public places such as workplaces or schools.

Chapter 15

How to Stop Overthinking with Positive Self-Talk

What Is self-talk?

Self-talk is the inner discussion that you have with yourself. Everybody engages in self-talk. However, the impact of self-talk is only evident when you are using it in a positive way. The power of self-talk can lead to an overall boost in your self-esteem and confidence. Moreover, if you convince your inner-self that you are beyond certain emotions, then you will also find it easy to overcome emotions that seem to weigh you down. If you can master the art of positive self-talk, you will be more confident about yourself and this can transform your life in amazing ways.

You can't be sure that you will always talk to yourself positively. Therefore, it is important to understand that self-talk can go in both directions. At times, you will find yourself reflecting on negative things. In other cases, you will think about the good things that you have achieved. Bearing this in mind, it is imperative that you practice positive self-talk. This can be understood as pushing yourself to think positively even when you are going through challenges.

If your self-talk is always inclined to think negatively, it doesn't mean that there is nothing you can do about it. With regular practice, you can shift your negative thinking into positive thinking. In time, this will transform you into a more optimistic person that is full of life.

Importance of positive self-talk

Research shows that positive self-talk can have a positive impact on your general wellbeing. The following are other benefits that you can get by regularly practicing positive self-talk.

Boosts your confidence

Do you often feel shy when talking to other people? Maybe you don't completely believe in your skills and abilities. Well, positive self-talk can transform the perceptions that you have about yourself and your abilities. Negative self-talk can hold you back from achieving things in life. It can even prevent you from even trying in the first place. Unfortunately, this can drive you to overthink about the things that you feel as though you should do. So, instead of acting, you end up wasting your time overthinking about them.

Positive self-talk lets you put aside any doubts that you could have about accomplishing a particular goal. Therefore, you will be motivated to act without worrying whether you will succeed or not. You're simply optimistic about life. There is nothing that can stop you from trying your best when attending to any activity.

Saves you from depression

Overthinking can make you more susceptible to depression because you garner the perception that you are incapable of performing well. Frankly, this affects your emotional and physical wellbeing. Some of the effects that you will experience when you're depressed include lack of sleep, lethargy, loss of appetite, nervousness, etc. Positive self-talk has the ability to change all of this. It will fill you with the optimism that you need to see past your challenges. As a result, instead of believing that you can't do it, you will begin to convince yourself that you can do it. Positive self-talk can transform how you feel, it's just a matter of changing how you perceive the world around you.

Eliminates stress

There are many stressors that we have to overcome every day. The truth is that we all go through stress. The only difference is how we deal with stress. Some people allow stress to overwhelm them. Often, you will find such folks with a negative outlook on life. They will have all sorts of negative comments about life. "Life is hard," "I can't take it anymore," "I'm always tired," "Things never get easier," etc. We've heard such comments coming from our friends who have given up on life. The reality is that stress can get the best of you if you surrender. Practicing positive self-talk can help you realize that stress comes and goes. It is a common thing that everybody experiences.

Protects your heart

We all know that stress is not good for our health. Stress leads to many diseases including cardiovascular diseases such as stroke. Therefore, by practicing positive self-talk, you will be protecting your heart.

Boost your performance

Positive self-talk can also help boost your performance in anything that you do. There are times when you find yourself feeling tired and dejected. For instance, when you wake up in the morning feeling as though you ran several kilometers, this can be draining. It affects how you attend to your daily activities. With positive self-talk, you can tap into your energy reserves and boost your performance. It is surprising how you can quickly change how you feel by thinking positively.

How positive self-talk works

Before getting into detail about practicing self-talk, it is important to understand how negative thinking works. There are several ways in which you can think negatively, including:

- Personalizing

This form of negative thinking occurs when you blame yourself for anything bad that happens to you.

- Catastrophizing

If you expect the worst to happen to you, then you are simply catastrophizing everything. The issue here is that you don't allow logic to help you understand that some things are not the way you think.

- Magnifying

Here, you pay more attention to negative things. In most cases, you will block your mind from thinking positively about any situation that you might be going through.

- Polarizing

You look to extremes when it comes to judging the things that are happening around you. From the perceptions that you have developed in your mind, something is either good or bad.

Tips for practicing positive self-talk

Have a purpose

There is a good reason why you will hear most people argue that it is important to live a purposeful life. Undeniably, when you strongly believe that you are here on this earth for a good reason, you will strive to be the best version of yourself. You will be constantly motivated to try to achieve your goals in life. The best part is that you will feel good about your accomplishments. This is because they are an indication that you are heading in the right direction towards your goals. Therefore, when practicing self-talk, always look to a higher purpose that you yearn to achieve. This will keep you on the move without worrying too much about the number of times you stumble.

Get rid of toxic people

It is common to have a bad day. We cannot deny the fact that there are times when life seems difficult. Usually, this happens when our emotions overwhelm us. Despite this fact, there are people who have these bad days every day. They never seem to stop talking about their worst experiences. Unfortunately, this can take a negative toll on your life, especially when interacting with other people. Picture a scenario where you are always told about how life is difficult. Your friend keeps mentioning to you that life has changed and it's impossible for you to realize your dreams. In time, this is the mindset that you will also develop. There is nothing good that you will see in your life since you can't think positively. The interesting thing is that you might actually be making positive changes, but you will unlikely notice.

Never compare yourself to others

It is easy to compare yourself to other people more so when you feel that you lack something. Sadly, such comparisons only push you to look down on yourself. The comparison game will blind you from seeing the valuable qualities that you have. You will develop a negative attitude towards your abilities as you assume that other people are better than you. By expressing how you are thankful for what you have, you can identify the numerous things that make you different from other people. This is a great way of developing your personality and helping you believe in yourself.

Talk positively with other people

Talking positively with other people will have an impact on your self-talk. If you constantly talk about negative things with those around you, then there is a likelihood that you will also engage in negative self-talk. There are probably numerous times where you've heard people say that you become what and how you think. Therefore, if you keep focusing on the negative, expect negativity to flow through your mind. Stop this by trying your best to surround yourself with positivity, starting with the way you talk to other people.

Believe in your success

The best way of propelling yourself to succeed in your endeavors is by believing that you can do it. If you don't believe that you can do it, then this holds you back from trying anything. This should be applied to everything you do. For example, if you are working towards losing weight, you should convince yourself that you can do it. This is the first step that will give you the energy you need to overcome challenges on your way to success.

Overcome the fear of failure

Succeeding in life also demands that you should overcome the fear of failure. You should always bear in mind that your failures are learning lessons. In fact, most people who have succeeded in life have failed at some point. When you overcome the fear of failure, you will be more than willing to try anything without hesitation. This opens doors to plenty of opportunities. The good news is that you will have learned a lot from the experience of failing.

Use positive affirmations

You can also give a positive boost to your self-talk by using positive affirmations. The best way to use these affirmations is by writing them down. Note them somewhere you can easily view them. For instance, you can stick them on your refrigerator or on your vision board, if you have one. The importance of positioning them in a convenient place is to guarantee that you motivate yourself every day. Ideally, this is an effective strategy of training your mind to always think positively. Examples of positive affirmations that you can note down include:

- I am blessed.
- I am a successful person.
- I embrace what life offers me.
- I am happy today.
- I allow myself to be filled with joy.

Avoid dwelling in the past

When you think too much about the past, it will likely be difficult to focus on the present. This will have an impact on your self-talk. If you keep regretting the mistakes that you have made, there is a good chance that you will think negatively. Your emotions will blind you from thinking clearly. As such, this can have an impact on the decisions you make.

It is imperative that you find a balance between thinking about the future and the present. When thinking about your future, focus on the positive. If there is something that you want, think in that direction and convince yourself that you already have it.

Chapter 16

How to Solve Worry Problems?

How much is too much?

It is very normal to experience worries, anxiety and doubts in daily life. It is our reaction to it which makes the greatest difference in our lives. It's very natural to get worked up about a first date, an upcoming interview, or an unpaid bill. Becoming frequently worried becomes overwhelming when it is uncontrollable and persistent. If every day you become worked up by picture all of the negative things that might happen to you, you are letting anxious thoughts interfere with your life and well-being.

Negative thoughts, incessant worrying, and constantly expecting poor outcomes will have a negative effect on your physical and emotional well-being. It gradually weakens you emotionally, taking your strength and leaving you restless and nervous, with headaches, insomnia, muscle tension and stomach problems.

The effect of this on your personal life, your concentration at school and work cannot be overemphasized. For some people, it's easier to take out their frustration on your loved ones and people closest to them, take alcohol or drugs or try to distract themselves by tuning out from everything.

Chronic anxiety and worry is a sign of Generalized Anxiety Disorder (GAD), a disorder that causes restlessness, nervousness and tension, together with a feeling of unease which can take over your life.

If you feel burdened by tension and worries, you can take a few steps to take your mind off anxious thoughts. Over time, worrying constantly becomes a problem. It becomes a mental habit when prolonged and is very difficult to break. Train your brain to be calm and think only positive thoughts, and change your outlook on life to a more relaxed and confident perspective.

How to quit worrying?

Tip 1: Choose a short period each day to worry

It can be quite difficult to be productive when your thoughts are consumed by worry and anxiety, distracting your attention from school, work, or your family. In this case, the strategy of putting off worrying can actually do a lot of good. Instead of getting rid of these thoughts, grant yourself permission to have these thoughts later on in your day.

Dedicate a period for worry each day. Set up a time and place to think of things that bother you. It should be at the same time every day (for example, 6 p.m. to 6:15 p.m. in the bedroom). Choosing a timeframe that won't affect your bedtime and or create additional anxiety in your life. During this period, you can worry about whatever you want. The rest of the day should be classified as worry-free.

Put down your worries in writing. When you find yourself thinking anxious or worrying thoughts, simply note them briefly and continue with your daily activities. Always remind yourself that there's time for you to think about it later; there is no need to get worked up about them now.

Take a look at your worry list during your scheduled worry period. If your thoughts still bother you, let yourself think about those things, but only for your specified worry period. You'll notice that, as you examine your worries in this manner, it's easier to establish a more balanced outlook to worrying. If, at this point, your worries don't seem as important as they used to, simply reduce the length of your worry period and enjoy your day to the fullest.

Tip 2: Challenge anxious thoughts

The way that you look at the world may be altered a bit if you are a chronic worrier and thinker. It changes everything, and you may tend to feel threatened. For instance, you picture only a worst-case scenario, and you assume the worst or handle your anxious thoughts as if they were facts.

As a result, you may not feel secure enough to tackle daily challenges head-on; you may assume that you'll lose it at the slightest sign of trouble. Such thoughts, also known as cognitive distortions, include: "All-or-nothing" thinking, having a black-and-white perspective, concluding that "If it isn't perfect, then I'm a complete failure," or "I wasn't hired for this job; I'll never get any job again." You may make a generalization from just one negative experience and expect it to be true forever. Life doesn't work that way.

You may notice only the things that went wrong in your day, instead of things that went well, resulting in thoughts such as: "I didn't get the last test question; I'm stupid, and I can't do anything right.." You may attribute positive events to sheer luck, rather than your own ability to create positive outcomes.

You may take your assumptions for facts. You may make yourself a mind-reader or fortune teller with thoughts like: "I just know something bad will happen" or "I know she secretly hates me." This creates bad energy. Without faith, your mind may automatically jump to worst-case scenarios, such as: "The plane is experiencing turbulence; it's going to crash." You may take your thoughts for reality: "I feel so stupid; I'm the laughingstock now."

You may make a list of your dos and don'ts and beat yourself up when you default on any of the rules, with thoughts such as, "I shouldn't have gone there. Now I look like such a fool." You may label yourself based on your shortcomings and mistakes, with thoughts such as, "I can't do anything right; I should be a loner." You may take responsibility for things that are beyond your control, thinking: "It's my fault my son died. I shouldn't have left him alone by the pool."

Challenging These Thoughts

Try this out. Challenge these negative thoughts during your worry period, and ask yourself these questions:

- What evidence proves that these thoughts are valid or not?

- Is there a better way to look at this situation? A better and more positive way?
- What are the chances of my fears becoming a reality? What are the probabilities? What are some likely outcomes in this situation?
- Are these thoughts helpful? How do they affect me? Do they help me or hurt me?
- What's my advice to a friend who has been in a similar situation?

Tip 3: Differentiate the solvable worries from the unsolvable worries

Studies have shown that you experience less anxiety when you worry. While you think about the problem in your head, you're distracted from your emotions for a while and feel like you're actually solving a problem; in reality, getting worried and problem-solving are two different things altogether.

By problem-solving, you are examining a situation, thinking of solid ways to deal with it, and putting these plans into action. On the other hand, worrying seldom leads to any solutions. The more time that you spend thinking of worst-case scenarios, the less prepared that you are to handle them if they actually happen. That's the simple truth.

Is your worry solvable?

There are different types of worries; some have solutions, while others don't. Solvable worries are those that you can act to resolve instantly. For instance, when you're preoccupied with your debts, you can call a friend or relative to settle your debts, with the option to repay them later.

This type of worry can also be described as productive worry. On the other hand, those worries that do not have a corresponding action can be characterized as unsolvable problems; for instance, thoughts like: What if I get leukemia someday? What if my family gets involved in an accident?

In a situation where you can take action about the thing getting you worried, begin to look for solutions. Compile a list of all the ways you feel that you can solve your worry. Don't get caught in searching for the one perfect answer to the problem.

Concentrate on those things within your reach that can be changed instead of brooding over situations that are out of reach. After deciding upon the solution that will solve your problem, develop an action plan. Immediately you set out to address your fear; you will be less worried.

On the other hand, when the worry is not something you can solve, make peace with yourself by being at ease with the uncertainty. For people who worry excessively, many of their fears tend to be along these lines. People tend to worry when they are trying to anticipate the future, and this is done to feel more in control and prevent potential problems.

However, the bitter truth is that worrying doesn't solve anything; life is occasionally unpredictable. So why not enjoy your life now instead of being engrossed in unpleasant things that have not taken place?

Most people long for inner peace: the feeling that everything is, and will be, all right. But sometimes, we worry, develop fears, and ponder the same things over and over without finding a way out.

The tragic thing is that, of course, we know rationally that the upcoming test is not a life-and-death situation. Our child is probably not lying in the ditch just because he/she does not call at the agreed-upon time. Our dull headache is probably harmless and not the symptom of a brain tumor.

Tip 4: Interrupt the worry cycle

Answer the following questions:

- What am I worried about?
- What possible solutions exist?
- Which solution should I choose?
- How and when do I implement the solution?

Just writing down your worries can provide you with some relief. If you then also write down different solutions, you will see your fears in a different light. You will adopt the observer perspective and will be able to think more logically about what you can do.

Meditate. Meditation helps to alleviate daily worries by shifting our attention. We focus only on the here and now and can leave the concerns of the past or future behind. Similarly, meditation can also help us observe ourselves and understand our negative thought patterns. We only need to find a comfortable, quiet place and focus carefully on our breathing. Various studies have shown that meditating not only helps to ease worries but can also reduce stress and anxiety.

Practice progressive muscle relaxation. Sports and exercise also promote relaxation and sleep. They also help to distract us from our everyday worries and promote our self-esteem and well-being. This confidence will make it easier for us to address our worries head-on. Also, researchers claim that exercise can reduce not only anxiety but also improve our emotional well-being and energy. Many scientists believe that physical activity can significantly reduce depression.

Tip 5: Talk about your worries.

One way to worry less is to talk to our closest friends about what is bothering us. When we are worried, friends can help us to alleviate our fears and see things from a different perspective. They can help us to look at the problem from the outside. Then, we can often find a solution or come to realize that it's not as bad a problem as we feared. When they listen without judgment or criticism and pay attention to what we say, their empathy can help us to feel calmer and more relaxed.

Having someone listen to us with empathy is essential to make us feel better. Even professional help is very beneficial, in some cases, if you cannot find a way out yourself.

Chapter 17
Reframing Your Negative Thoughts

Like anyone on this planet, there's as much time as you can to be happy. But you still don't have joy as your main priority, like most people. Or maybe you think you do, but in reality, you actively sabotage yourself by falling into depression, misery, remorse and other unproductive negative ideas.

However, it's very easy to fall into depression without joy as a goal and suffer more than you deserve in this lifetime. This is why it is so important if you want to know how to enhance the quality of your life, you'll accept happiness as your first goal and not just as a pleasant idea.

If you genuinely seek joy, you should be able to notice the negative and reframe it, and the right thinking is critical because you have thousands or tens of thousands of negative thoughts a day. You will wake up every day to battle demons–dispute, despair and depression. No other way. It is spiritual warfare and every day you must be prepared to wake up and fight.

The positive thing is having the right attitude, and you will start to feel better instantly. Have the right outcome. Better still, everyone can use this technology because it's not based on "objective truth." Reframing negativity does not depend on your wealth, or on your IQ or appearance, or on something else you want. You will make a big difference in the quality of your life from today with the right will and application of your imagination.

How to reframe negative thoughts?

- **AWARENESS**

Your awareness is the first thing to concentrate on. In other words, be wary of negative thoughts. If happiness is your first priority, you will take depressing consciousness very seriously, like a gun on your head.

You will be mindful of it and, at least every day, you will have thousands of negative thoughts. It is just a problem to capture them, to admit that you are frustrated and to ask the right questions.

- **Ask the right questions**

Both combinations of:

- Why am I unhappy?
- What do I do to feel better?

You are the questions you pose, and you know how to make the right questions. This is really necessary. If you ask the right questions, the right reframe is what you want.

- **REFRAMING**

The correct reframe is the only reframe at the moment. You may not be satisfied, but you can still get out of doubt, frustration and depression— even when it's just optimistic.

The most valuable skill in practice is reframing or state management which is much more successful than any form of therapy. Because counseling deals with the past, the past does not exist anymore. The present is all that is true and policy management regulates the present.

The past, the present and the future are not the way forward. You suffer because you stay trapped in the past.

It's like physical pain, except it's not that bad, from fever to cancer. Once the pain is gone, after you have tried, you can't remember physical pain. However, emotional suffering can be restored, renewed and remembered forever. It is supported by many forms of therapy!

Compare mind to body:

- Therapy is like having a physical wound or injury which causes you to suffer and pick and open and dig into it, thus raising pain so that you recognize pain, and somehow "process it." Compare the mind with the body.
- The reframing, in order to remove the discomfort and feel good at the moment, takes the same actual skull or fracture that causes you pain and takes the right treatment.
- The realization that changes the game comes when you know that you get how you feel.
- Negative thinking will only harm you if you accept it.
- It doesn't matter how bad your feelings are or what has happened to you, you just decide how you feel.

- You can choose positive or negative and you are actually CHOOSING when you are negative.

Different types of reframes

You have to learn two types of reframes to have better positive thinking:

- Unproductive negative thoughts that are pessimistic and purposeless feelings.
- Negative proposals that require practice. These are not even the enemy's negative thoughts. They either alert you to thought changes, or they warn about habits that you have to change.

Reframing unproductive negative thoughts

- **IGNORE**

For low-level negative feelings, the safest reframe is always to forget it. Forget it. Thoughts like you're a loser or sick of going to work–just like a nervous man at the pub, you talk to them. No or I'm a stupid or distracted.

- **Changing focus**

Change of emphasis is an ideal way to reframe negativity. The easiest change of focus is about going back to work. When I think negative during the day, my reframe just goes back to my goal. In minutes I'll have totally forgotten the feeling. One perfect way to signal a shift of emphasis is to define and continue thinking as unproductive.

Reframing negative thoughts which requires action

- Positive reframe

For feelings that need a change of mind, it is a positive reframe that your best move is. I hated it every minute when I was in sales from my managers to dealing with rude customers to cold calls to colleagues. That's when I reframed every move and every cold call to make more money, and the money will be saved. And I use this money to fund my enterprises and to avoid wage slavery forever.

If I changed my mind, I could not only excel but turned a big negative into a constructive one. I was actually able to escape, and I was able to monetize my experience by writing a book on how to market it.

One important thing to note is to check the reframes while doing a constructive reframing. Some guys teaching NLP-based pickups teach people to think of themselves as supermen or 10 feet as they approach women. It's not a useful structure, because your subconscious mind would never buy.

Some guys teach the method to approach women in order to make them feel wanted. It is a good thing, and it is a good thing that you can honestly express your purpose but moving around in 2000 is a challenge. Nonetheless, I saw some guys on the pickup boards thinking about their ability and making 2000 females feel desired. This is not a positive reframe.

If you meet a woman, it will be your final game to get this woman and concentrate on the outcome. Under these cases, you have to look at doing something to improve your sexual market interest and make major behavioral improvements.

Ultimately, it's a safe idea to sit down and talk about the most consistent destructive trends. If it is illness, fear of death, or low self-esteem, the development of optimistic reframe can take place. Others will go back and forth when the big negative feedback loops become nasty minds, which they are.

- **Behavioral change**

The behavioral shift is the perfect reframe for negative thinking about problems in your life, whether they are addictions, unpleasant individuals, or choices in lifestyle or a work you dislike. Such kinds of negative thoughts should be listened to and followed up by your peers. Hearing these kinds of thoughts and applying approaches will be the bulk of your personal development success.

One approach that might be useful when it comes to negative behaviors is to sit down and list the 10 worst recurring issues. From a work you don't want to what your 10 biggest problems are and action-based solutions can be found. I did it myself and it was a huge step forward. I have actually created a system with the Wunderlist task management app to solve those problems by setting my mission, priorities, schedules and tasks.

Chapter 18
How to Use Meditation to Deal with Overthinking?

Meditation is an easy and logical step for any empath. It can be very uncomfortable, at first, to sit quietly all alone with your thoughts. Try to remember that the purpose of meditation is to let those thoughts and emotions come, and then release them. Allow them to wash over you the way waves move over your feet when you walk along the seashore, crashing up and then quickly, gently, fading away.

You can also meditate on specific subjects or questions that you struggle to comprehend. The purpose of meditation is not to stir anxiety, though, so if you note repetitive, obsessive, or negative thought patterns, you may want to change your approach before your next session.

If you are already well-practiced in meditation, you might want to further challenge yourself and awaken your third eye chakra by challenging your thought patterns. Some metaphysical guides suggest using inquisition to aid this process, continually answering each of your thoughts with the question: "Is that true?" If that method feels combative or sparks feelings of internal conflict, you can instead practice disbelieving your thoughts, entertaining the possibility that the truth is the opposite of what you perceive it to be.

Create a safe haven

To ensure that self-care becomes a regular part of your new routine, you'll want to make space for it in your life--literally. Even if it has to be inside a closet, make sure you find some space to create a safe haven for yourself. You could also think of it as a peace bubble, meditation space, or a spiritual altar. The idea is to create an ideal space in which to center yourself whenever life outside this haven starts to feel overwhelming. You may want to fill it with candles and crystals, smudge sticks, plants, cozy pillows, and blankets. If you relish the endless potential of a blank slate, your haven might be completely bare, dark, and quiet. There is no right or wrong way, only the way that feels right for you.

De-Clutter and organize your living space

Now that you've created a safe haven, your next goal should be to arrange the rest of your living space in a way that helps you to feel balanced, organized, efficient, and at peace. Even if you don't consider yourself a visual or materially oriented person, the way your home looks matters; it is the first thing your eyes see every morning when you wake up, and the last thing you see before you fall asleep at night. Its appearance makes a mark on your dreams and subconscious world, as well as on your conscious thought processes. Furthermore, the way it smells, sounds, and feels is important, too.

If you find the theories of Feng Shui resonate with you, then go ahead and evaluate the layout of your home and furniture, and rearrange whatever you have to in order to respect its principles. This is especially recommended for geomantic empaths--Feng Shui is also sometimes called "geomancy," and it addresses the same energetic frequencies that geomantic empaths are attuned to.

If there's no time for a full interior redecoration effort, then instead, you may want to focus on clearing unwanted energy from your living space. Take a mental inventory of the items on display in your home. How many of them were items you chose based on desire? How many did you choose based on necessity? Be on the lookout for gifts you've received, and remind yourself that you are alone and no one is judging you before you ask yourself: how do I really feel about these items that were given to me? Do they have sentimental value and represent a feeling of love and affection for me? Or, were some of them given by people who were trying to manipulate or influence my behaviors? Do some of them remind me that people in my life don't actually get me or understand who I am?

If so, don't feel ashamed for acknowledging it. Sometimes, gifts are not given from a place of generosity, but in an attempt to exert willpower. Recognize these items in your home as centers of negative or stagnant energy, and give yourself permission to dispose of them, give them away, or send them to remote storage.

Yoga, tai chi, and physical mindfulness practice

Exercise is undoubtedly good for the body and soul, but it can be even more effective when combined with mindfulness. Mindfulness is the concept of heightening our awareness of things we usually take for granted or have learned to ignore, like our breathing or thought patterns. Yoga is especially popular, as it addresses the need for physical alignment and mindfulness, promoting focus, relaxation, acceptance, and self-love. It can also be tailored easily to suit many different needs, sometimes fully embracing its spiritual element, or at other times being exclusively concerned with the physical body. You can easily find a yoga class to attend, and there are many schools of yoga to choose from, depending on your desire to enhance strength, find balance, repair injury, or find deeper relaxation. You can also practice alone in your home or outdoors in nature.

Tai chi also stimulates mindfulness through a series of slow, controlled physical movements. Generally, yoga can pose more of a physical challenge, whereas Tai chi requires a great deal of patience and focus, so it challenges the mind. It also looks more like a dance form, so those who feel freed by creative expression may prefer tai chi to other similar practices.

Grounding

Grounding is theoretically easy, but will only be as effective as the amount of energy you channel into the practice. All you need to do is remove your shoes and socks, plant your feet on the ground (ideally in a place where you feel a strong connection to nature), and imagine you are growing roots like a tree. Many empaths will close their eyes, breathe deeply, and utilize some form of meditation or affirmation during their grounding practice.

One mantra that you might find useful is the alternating repetition of two phrases: first, "I am one with the universe," where you may substitute the word "universe" with "all things" or the name of a higher power in your faith; and secondly, "I am distinct, unique, powerful and purposeful." These two phrases articulate polarized sentiments that many empaths mentally seesaw back and forth between; the goal here is to honor both ideas as part of the same universal truth.

Some empaths find this practice especially powerful near oceans, historical landmarks, or sites of natural phenomena, like volcanoes or earthquakes. Grounding is highly recommended for geomantic and precognitive empaths.

Dietary changes

Every living being, whether plant, animal or human, is made of energy. So, if you are consistently consuming foods that carry forms of negative energy, it can manifest in your body as chronic pain, illness, malnourishment, or even as an emotional symptom, like depression.

An elimination diet is a simple way to effect major change in your personal energy field, and it usually provokes rapid change. You may be very surprised to find aches or points of tension are suddenly released, despite the fact that you never even noticed them before they were flushed away.

Intermittent fasting can also be a useful tool to enhance mental clarity, though it should be done with caution. Those who lead highly active lifestyles or suffer from nutritional imbalances may find this practice dangerous.

Affirmations and manifestation exercises

Have you ever had the experience of feeling overwhelmed by a mental to-do list, only to write it out on paper or tell someone else about it, and suddenly realize that it's easily doable, and not worth stressing over?

Or, have you ever felt that a dream or wish was too far out of reach to entertain--but then, by declaring it aloud, you suddenly felt it drawn closer to you, fully within reach?

This is a manifestation in action. Whether you intend to address it or not, the universe is listening to you, so proclaiming your desires and self-esteem clearly can have an amazing ripple effect on your life. It can amplify your confidence, strengthen your resolve, encourage feelings of gratitude, and help you to maintain positive energy. Just be sure to project your truth without distortion, and be careful not to ask the universe for anything you aren't prepared to receive.

Use verbal or written affirmations during any self-love practice (yoga, meditation, bathing, or even while getting dressed in the morning, if you are pressed for time) to encourage self-love, drive motivation, and stay focused on your personal goals and values. Manifestation will be more focused on the future, whereas affirmations influence your current perceptions of reality. Remember that our thoughts shape our realities, so the simple act of reframing negative thoughts through the language of gratitude can change your entire outlook on life.

Journaling

There is no right or wrong way to use this practice. Regular free-writing is a fantastic way to find greater clarity of thought, as well as to self-soothe unexpressed frustrations or concerns. It may also be helpful to read over past entries from time to time, like a detective, whenever you suspect interference from a phantom source of negativity in your energy field. Journaling will help you to note healthy and risky patterns in your own behavior, as well as within the framework of your interpersonal relationships. It will also be cathartic, helping you to let go of negative feelings and leave them sealed in the past.

Chapter 19

Returning to Self-Care

It is important to take care of yourself while you are trying to recover from overthinking and anxiety. This means you have got to relax. For people with anxiety, it can feel almost impossible because it has probably been a long time since they have felt relaxed. In fact, it can be unsettling to feel relaxed for them because it is unfamiliar. The longer you ignore your need for self-care goes on, the direr it will get. If you don't have the time to relax, you can at least tide yourself over until you can focus on yourself. If you are feeling tired at work, close your eyes for just a few minutes.

Check how you are doing physically because your physical and mental health goes hand in hand. It's easy to not be feeling well for a long time and not realize it or push it to the back of your priority list because you are trying to push through and get through the days.

As an overthinker, you probably spend much of your day grappling with a multitude of worries. Arrange a certain time in the evening where you put away your worries until tomorrow. Save them for a time when you can actually have an impact on them. Also, figure out the ones that are necessary and the ones that do nothing for you but cause you stress.

Overthinkers are masters at borrowing trouble. They can create problems for themselves that do not have to exist. For example, if your car is having trouble, you can give yourself a panic attack thinking of how expensive it could wind up being and worrying about if the car is even fixable. Find out how much the repairs cost first. Go on the assumption that whatever is wrong with the car will be fixable. Think about it this way. If it does turn out to be something serious, by the time you get to the point where you find out this information, you will have worried yourself into a frazzle. This means you will have rendered yourself completely ineffective and unable to figure out how to get yourself out of the situation you have worried so much about. No amount of stressing out can prevent a situation. It only takes energy away from you. If you do not give yourself a panic attack about it, then you will be able to take on the situation while you are still fresh.

You need to redirect your thoughts about the situation. Instead of going to "this is the worst thing that could ever happen" or "this is going to ruin my life," focus on this thought instead: "What is the first step I need to take to get myself out of this situation?" Don't even trouble yourself with the overall solution at first. Just think about how you are going to get through today. Think about paying off the immediate amount.

Let's think about what it means to practice self-care. It could be argued that the root of self-care is getting proper sleep. Every other aspect of your life will take a hit if you are not sleeping well. The timing of your sleep is just as important as the number of hours you get. Let's say you don't fall asleep until 4 in the morning. You probably won't wake up until around noon, so you've already lost half of your day. You will still be groggy, and it'll probably take you longer yet to get out of bed, and even then, you will feel a very low level of energy. It will be all you can do just to get the bare minimum done.

You need to put away your phone before you go to bed. If you don't, there will be a few problems. For one, you will be tempted to play around on your phone and check your social media newsfeeds, and it is easy to lose track of time when you do this. You might look up, and it's 1 in the morning. Then you will need time to fall asleep because no one does the minute they close their eyes.

Do not bring up heavy or upsetting discussion topics late in the evening. If it hasn't come up by then, and no one's life is in danger, it can wait until the morning. Big discussions tend to take an hour to resolve, two if it's a particularly hefty one. If you started it at eight in the evening, you might not be done with it until nine or ten. Then you will have a hard time getting to sleep because when your mind is restless, your sleep will be fitful.

Self-care also means doing things that make you happy. Pick up a hobby. Remember, trying something out doesn't mean you have to stick with it forever. You can take one painting class, decide you don't like it, and never go to another one. Nothing will be lost from trying something.

You often hear "I need a mental health day" as a joke, but there is something to it. Sometimes in our daily lives, with all of our responsibilities, we can become burned out. Just like a cell phone needs its battery recharged, we need our mental battery recharged.

There is no right or wrong way to take a mental health day. It is all about what you want to do. During this type of day, you do not have any responsibilities, and you don't need to think about them. Only do things that make you feel good. It is advisable to avoid too much time on social media during a mental health day.

Establishing good habits for yourself is key to overcoming anxiety and overthinking. If you don't take care of yourself, your defenses are compromised. You are more prone to having physical illnesses, and you will not feel as good about yourself. This means taking pride in your appearance.

Putting effort into your appearance doesn't mean you have to dress in ways that are not you. If you are a woman who doesn't like to wear makeup, you don't have to start doing it. You can look perfectly fine without wearing anything you don't feel comfortable with. In fact, it is cautioned against to try to do that. Then you will feel self-conscious and like everyone is staring at you, which will be the catalyst for an overthinking episode.

What it means to take care of your appearance is to put time and effort into it. When we get into ruts of depression and anxiety, we have a tendency to press the snooze button as many times as possible. Then, when there is no more time to lie in bed, we'll get ready as quickly as we can, and it will be a blur. This means there's no thought put into what you are going to wear, and there's no time to fix your hair other than to run through it a couple of times with a brush. You might not even have time to take a look at yourself in the mirror before you go. This is demoralizing because you know you are not looking for your best and are worried others will notice. It will inhibit your confidence when talking to others and might even prevent you from talking to others.

Some people like to pick out what they are going to wear the next morning. This can help you feel more prepared for the next day and gives you one last thing to think about in the morning. Then you have more time to dedicate to other aspects of your appearance. Create some sort of skin ritual. You will start to see results quickly. Learn about different things you can do with your hair and find out what hairstyles work the best with your face shape and which ones you find appealing.

Taking care of yourself also means taking care of the space around you. It is said that a cluttered room is a sign of a mind that has chaos going on inside of it. That is why de-cluttering your environment is so important. When your house is messy, you will feel uncomfortable inside of it. It can get to a point where you have to go through a lot of trouble to navigate in your own house because of the clutter. You have to walk around and step over things. It will increase your stress to have to go through an obstacle course just to walk around in your own home. It is depressing to look at a messy house because you are living in a space you are not pleased with. Instead of your house being a place to come to at the end of the day and find relief from as you leave your worries behind for the day, you come to see a place that has a chaotic energy and that you are ashamed of. You will avoid having any company over and you will dread when you have to let someone in your house, like a repairman, because you are worried about what they will think when they see the state of your house (this is not good for those who overthink, whose shame about the state of the house will last long beyond when the repairman leaves).

There is an impact the energy in the room can have on you. This does not have to carry a spiritual meaning. Have you ever almost gone to a restaurant, but you looked at the people you were with, and you all decided to leave and find somewhere else to go eat because there was something that felt weird about the place? That is what it means to have positive or negative energy. Sometimes it is called the "vibe" or "juju" a person or place gives off. When you have clutter in your house and have not managed its upkeep in a while, the place you live in will have negative energy. It will not be conducive to living a healthy lifestyle and being productive. The way you keep your house sets a tone for the way you live your life. If you regularly clean the space you live in, you will feel more confident about yourself. You will start to enjoy being at home.

There is something to the phrase "fake it until you make it." Even if you are faking it, you are choosing to dwell on something that is beneficial to you rather than something that is harmful. Have you ever been having a bad day, but one of your friends invited you to go out with them, and you decided to take them up on the offer? At first, it might have felt contrived to go out and pretend to be having fun. There was a part of you that wanted to keep wallowing in your sorrows. However, since you were hanging out with your friend and talking to them about things that were unrelated to whatever was bothering you, you didn't have time to devote all of your time to that. After a while, there came a point where you decided you'd rather have fun with your friend than think about what was upsetting you, most likely something you had little to no control over.

Chapter 20

The Key to Feeling Good

Being happy is so important, yet it's often overlooked. If you don't feel good, you won't feel as motivated to accomplish your goals. It will be harder to be driven and get to where you need to be, as you simply won't feel up to anything. Taking care of yourself is crucial. When you feel good, you may form better relationships with others and have people that can support you and have a good time with you. You can get more done, as you will actually want to improve yourself and succeed. You will be more confident in yourself because you'll be treating yourself the way that you should be and recognizing your worth instead of feeling sorry for yourself. It will be easier to succeed, achieve your goals, and have access to more opportunities.

Improving your mental health

Your mental health is so important, yet most people seem to forget that it even exists. You can go to the gym and eat as healthily as you'd like, yet that won't help you if your mental health is suffering. You must take some time to care for your mental health, as you can't be happy otherwise. There are a few ways that you can make an effort to improve your mental health, and you may incorporate some great habits into your life to better your mental health.

One way to improve your mental health is to practice self-care. Every day, take some time to care for yourself. You may do this a few ways, such as reading a book or relaxing. Find out what works best for you to help you calm down. It's important to make the effort to fully devote some time to yourself. It may even be as simple as lighting a candle and breathing. There are many ways that you can practice self-care, and it's important to find out what works best for you. Maybe you can even practice a new self-care activity every day! You may plan ahead for the upcoming month and pick simple ways for you to practice self-care. Perhaps you can do it for under thirty minutes every weekday and an hour or more on weekends. You may even choose one self-care item for each day of the week. Regardless, it's important to choose an activity that you genuinely enjoy and really go out of your way to take care of yourself. There are so many ways to practice self-care!

Another way to improve your mental health is by treating yourself well. Learn how to master self-compassion and self-esteem. Practice being more understanding with yourself and forgive yourself for making mistakes. Also, remember that you deserve happiness and success. Respect yourself and your decisions, and don't be so hard on yourself.

You may also work on improving your self-confidence. One great way to do this is by building your confidence. Set goals and accomplish them, even if they're small. Successes, no matter how small they are, will help you recognize that you are capable of success.

Practicing mindfulness is a great way to improve your mental health. When you are faced with a difficult situation, learn how to live in the moment. Focus on the present instead of worrying about what will happen in the future or what did happen in the past. If you live your life with regrets, you will never be able to move forward. Wasting your time on worrying will not help solve any of your problems. Instead, take time to appreciate the present for what it is.

Therapy can be a wonderful solution for bettering your mental health. If you have tried to help improve your mental health by yourself but haven't had luck, it may be time for you to seek help from someone else through therapy. Cognitive-behavioral therapy can be a great way to find solutions to your problems. Therapy can be especially helpful if you haven't had luck improving your mental health by yourself or if you feel like you have nobody to talk to. Therapy can give you an outside perspective on you.

Having a positive outlook

Having a positive outlook on life can really help you to be more positive and have an overall greater appreciation for life. You will be able to find joy in life instead of focusing on any negativity. When you can improve your mindset, your whole world will change. Your perspective can turn a bad situation into a good one. Learning to appreciate life can help you to be happier with how everything is going. A negative outlook on life can prevent you from making the most out of your life, and it can cause those around you to be unhappy as well. There are a few simple tips that you can use to change your perspective and have a more positive outlook.

You may start journaling. This can help you to feel like you're in more control of your life, and you may take it any direction that you'd like to. Perhaps you wish to write down what you're grateful for and the good aspects of life. You may also want to write down how you feel so that you can cope with it in a healthier way. Journaling is also great for writing down your goals and your progress toward accomplishing those goals.

Another way to have a more positive outlook is by focusing on the good. For every negative thing that you notice, you must also come up with two positive aspects of it. For instance, you may be stuck in traffic and get upset about being late. However, this can give you some time to call a friend that you haven't gotten the chance to talk to in a while and help you to take time to yourself. There are always positive aspects of every situation. It might just take a bit of effort to find them.

Similarly, you must view challenging situations and mistakes as beneficial to you. If you can learn to view life in the way that everything happens for a reason, you will be much better off. Instead of thinking that your life is ruined because you didn't get the job, know that there is a better job waiting out there for you that will be an even better fit for you. If you can't get past challenges, you'll never grow. You can't let mistakes or failures bring you down, as they are inevitable and will always be a part of your life.

It's important to change your mindset when it comes to change. Without change, you can't grow or improve. Although you may enjoy the risk-free aspect of comfort, it will not get you anywhere. Go for your goals! Chase your dreams! If you don't make the effort to take some risks, you won't get any further in life. Change can be frightening, but it's also very important. You'll never know if you like something until you try it, and it's okay to change your mind. Change is a blessing, not a curse. You must learn how to appreciate change instead of fearing it.

Improving your physical health

Your physical health is also important for your happiness. When your body is healthy, and you take care of it, you will be able to function the best. Taking care of your body can help you to have more energy and feel better overall. It can also help you to do more instead of being held back by your health. Taking care of your body will also help you to feel better about yourself. You will be able to realize that you are capable of taking care of yourself and doing what's best for yourself. You may feel more confident in your body and your ability to accomplish your goals.

First, you must get a proper amount of sleep. This is necessary for allowing you to function at your best and have a proper amount of energy. The amount of sleep that you need will depend on your age and personal preferences. However, it is very helpful to have a sleeping schedule. Going to bed and waking up at the same time every day can help your body to get used to sleeping for the proper amount. You may form routines to perform before going to bed and after waking up to really maximize this effect.

Eating properly is essential for taking care of your mental health. It is important to allow yourself to occasionally eat unhealthy foods, but you should eat an overall healthy diet. Portions are also very important, as eating the proper amount can help you to maintain an ideal weight. Eating at the same time each day can also improve your metabolic health. Determine when you would like to eat and how often you would like to eat. Making these simple changes can really help you to improve the way you eat.

Staying hydrated is also important for your health. You must get a proper amount of water each day to be at your best. One way to motivate yourself to do so is by getting a water bottle that looks nice. This can encourage you to drink from it more. You may even label the side with the hours of the day as a way to set hydration goals for yourself. Cutting out beverages besides water can really help you, especially since most other drinks contain excessive amounts of sugar. Caffeine and alcohol consumption should also be limited to obtain the best health possible.

Exercising is very important to keep your body healthy. You must choose activities that you enjoy. For some, this may very well be going to the gym. Others don't thrive in that environment and prefer to exercise by themselves. This may be running, swimming, walking, or biking. You may even try at-home workouts. Taking classes or lessons can be a great way to learn how to exercise a certain way. You may also involve yourself in sports or clubs. This is a great way to get out and workout, and you'll be able to meet others with similar interests.

Cultivating positive relationships

To improve your relationships with others, it's very important to surround yourself with the right people. Make sure that you are spending your time with people who motivate, inspire, and encourage you to live your best life possible. It is okay to say no to people, and you must learn to value yourself. Holding on to grudges will not get you anywhere, and it's important to eliminate the conflict that you have. You may also spend more time caring for others. When you put in the effort, others will start doing the same. Work on building positive relationships with those around you.

Feeling good can help you to live your best life. You're at your best when you are happy. It is possible to achieve happiness. You may do this by improving your mental health, which can allow you to think more clearly about the positivity in your life. Similarly, you may have a more positive outlook on life. Improving your physical health can make you feel better, both physically and mentally. You may also work on improving your relationships with others so that you can surround yourself with the right people that can support you and encourage you to be your best.

Chapter 21
Self-Discipline

Self-discipline is important. It can make a huge difference for you, and it can help you to stick to your habits. Instead of giving in to temptation, you will be able to control your actions and make the right choices to take care of yourself. This can be anything from dietary choices to resisting the urge to procrastinate. Although you can't deprive yourself of happiness, it's important to be able to discipline yourself so that you can make the right choices. Often, we get caught up in the domino effect of wrong choices. Once you make one wrong choice, you figure that you've already messed up, so you continue on that path and lose interest in taking care of yourself properly. Although you may allow yourself to give in to temptation every so often, it's important to be able to have an overall sense of self-discipline so that you can live your best life possible. You must learn how to practice self-discipline so that you can begin using it in your life. You may also learn how to control your thoughts and practice self-discipline mentally.

How to practice self-discipline

When you can practice self-discipline and self-control, you'll be much happier. You'll be able to achieve your goals without giving in to temptation. Self-discipline can improve many aspects of your life. You can improve your diet, save money, and accomplish whatever other goals you may have. It will help you to resist the urge to give in to bad habits and focus more on what matters to you in life. You won't be dragged down by certain impulses, feelings, or emotions. Your decision-making skills will improve, and you'll have greater control over your life. Additionally, you'll be happier with yourself and your life because you'll be doing what you want to instead of what others want you to. There are a few ways that you can improve your self-discipline skills and become better at practicing control over yourself. However, it will take practice and patience to master the skill of self-discipline.

First, you must identify and remove your weaknesses. If you are trying to improve your diet and know that your weakness is cookies, you shouldn't have cookies lying around your house within easy reach. Instead of denying what your weaknesses are, or put off getting over them, recognize what you struggle with. You won't be able to overcome your weaknesses until you recognize them. Identify what's getting in the way of achieving your goals. You must then make an effort to remove the temptations from your life. Additionally, you have to commit. You can't remove the chocolate chip cookies and shortly thereafter go to the store and buy sugar cookies. Remove your temptations, and keep them out of your life. You may also develop a further plan for your goals, outlining what you want to do and what you don't want to do. Come up with a path for you to follow so that you can achieve your goals.

You may practice improving your self-discipline. Go out of your way to make yourself uncomfortable. Instead of avoiding what makes you uncomfortable, just face your fears. The more that you're able to practice discomfort, the better you will be with it. This will also allow you to control yourself more and stop avoiding the unfamiliar. Your mindset will change, and you may even enjoy trying new things and doing what once was uncomfortable.

Remember to focus on one thing at a time. Instead of overwhelming yourself with a huge list of new habits to try, only focus on 1-3 goals at once. This will allow you to fully commit to them and focus on what truly matters to you. If you come up with a dozen goals to try at once, it won't be as effective. You likely won't remember to work on all of them at once, have the time to focus on them, or be able to commit to so many changes at once.

What self-discipline can help with

Self-discipline can help with many aspects of your life. Often, we associate it with diets. You may think of self-discipline when you imagine resisting junk foods or the like. However, it can help you with all areas of your life. You will become more productive, form better relationships, be a happier person, become more positive, accomplish more goals, and overall be a better person. It will take effort, though. You must be consistent with your actions and practice patience when it comes to self-discipline. You won't achieve results overnight, but you will become stronger with more practice and greater knowledge. Knowing how self-discipline can benefit, you can help you stay motivated to get on the path to being more disciplined.

Self-discipline is a practice of consistently. When you master the art of discipline, you will be able to be more consistent with your actions. It will require you to power through challenges and remain strong despite facing obstacles. You may practice consistency with both positive and negative actions. You will learn how to consistently avoid bad habits as well as consistently practicing good habits. By doing so, you allow yourself to fill your life with more of what matters most.

Self-discipline can help you to be a kinder and more emotionally stable person. You may practice self-discipline with your emotions and reactions. Instead of letting your mood influence them, you may discipline yourself. Often, we use life as an excuse for feeling upset or thinking a certain way. However, when you're in a negative mood, everything seems different. Your perspective of the world will completely flip, having you think that everything is wrong with life. If you can train yourself to acknowledge your moods and pause before reacting to them, you can save yourself a lot of hassle. Instead of overreacting for no reason, you may understand that you aren't in a good place mentally. This will not be an optimal time for you to make decisions or complete important tasks. Know when to stop yourself, and you may prevent negativity. Pause before reacting to your emotions. Pause before saying something that you'll later regret. This can help you tremendously.

Your relationships with others will also improve. When you practice self-discipline, you will follow through with plans. You won't make plans or say yes to plans that you know you won't follow through with. You won't over-commit yourself. You will also understand the importance of dependability, and you won't let small issues get in the way. Self-discipline also goes hand-in-hand with honesty, loyalty, and integrity. When you can control yourself, you will stay true to your values and act according to them. People will respect and appreciate you for it.

Self-discipline can also help you to achieve your goals. In order for you to accomplish your goals, you must stay committed to them. It's important for you to remain motivated despite any obstacles that you may face. There will be challenges, yet you must be able to stick through them.

Decisions and discipline

When you're disciplined, you will also be able to make better decisions. Instead of giving in to temptation, you will choose the path to success. It will be easier to make choices that align with your goals, and you'll be able to stick with them. You won't let others get in the way of your success or influence you otherwise. It will be up to you. Small issues won't bother you, and you'll still be able to make the right choices. It may be easier for you to plan out your goals and commit to a decision as well. Self-discipline can help you to solve your problems.

When you build better habits, you are already making better decisions. Self-discipline will allow you to create good and healthy habits that you'll stick to. This can eliminate the potential for making bad decisions, as you will have already made the choice beforehand. For instance, you may plan out your diet and what you want to eat. One who masters self-discipline will stick to that diet and resist temptation. This will make the choice for you of what to eat, and you won't have to feel guilty about going against this choice in the future.

You will also accomplish more goals that you want to accomplish. One who is disciplined will have their goals written out and prioritized. They will accomplish what they want to. You won't have to make as much of a choice on what you want to do, as you will have already planned that out. You will also make better decisions in regards to your productivity. Instead of choosing to procrastinate or give in to distractions, you will make the right choice. A disciplined individual will realize that it's better to get all of your work done before you play. When you procrastinate, you still have the task hanging over you. Yet, getting everything done first will allow you to fully enjoy your fun without feeling the stress of what you should be doing instead.

In general, the decision-making process will be better. When you learn to control your reactions, you will become less impulsive. Although it is good to be spontaneous every so often, the wisest decisions require some thought beforehand. You may weigh your options and reach the proper conclusion with time. However, this requires you to practice patience.

Discipline can help you to overcome laziness. Instead of making the choice to avoid work or not do the right thing because you aren't in the mood for it, you will recognize the importance of pushing through and accomplishing what you must. The easier option is not usually the option that leads to success. In fact, success takes hard work. You have to face challenges. You will make mistakes. Rejection will occur. Others may not fully support you and believe in you. However, those that succeed have great discipline. They recognize that success will take hard work, and they're willing to put in that work and suffer now to achieve results later.

Self-discipline can make a huge impact on you. It will help you to learn how to practice it, as you can help yourself to achieve your goals. You may also learn how to practice self-control over your thoughts, which will influence your behavior, feelings, and actions. Self-discipline can help you improve many aspects of your life, and you may form better habits while avoiding unhealthy temptations. You'll be much happier with yourself and realize your full potential. Additionally, your decision-making skills will improve, and you'll be able to make choices that have the best possible effect on your life.

Chapter 22
Goal Setting

Setting goals goes hand-in-hand with time management. You cannot claim that you are good at managing time when you lack goals. It is important to stop and question yourself about how you set your goals. Are you the type of person who sets big goals and takes massive steps toward achieving these goals? Or rather, are you one of those individuals who opt to set SMART goals and develop practical measures to meet them? Without a doubt, there are plenty of theories out there about setting goals. Therefore, it can be easy to get blown by the wind if you don't know what is right for you.

One of the main reasons that people set goals is to increase their productivity. This means that more work will be successfully completed in less time. So, having goals implies that you will be managing your time well. This discussion aims to take you through goal setting in time management. Through the information delivered in this, you will be better placed to create realistic goals that are measurable and time-bound.

Essential principles in setting goals

Most people set goals for anything that they plan to do. Often, we find ourselves planning for the day even without our knowledge. If you have developed a habit of setting goals, it will not be difficult for you to list some of the things that you wish to achieve in the next two months or one year. However, this is where most of us go wrong. Goal setting is not just about deciding what you want. There is more to this than what we actually understand. According to professors Gary Latham and Edwin Locke, there is a science behind the entire concept of setting goals (Casano, 2019). This is what influenced them to write A Theory of Goal Setting and Task Performance, which features the following principles of goal setting. These principles are succinctly deliberated in the following paragraphs.

Clarity

This is the first principle, which defines whether your goal is effective or not. Just as the name suggests, your goal ought to be clearly defined. A clear goal should be one that you can picture yourself reaching. You should find it easy to envision yourself after achieving the goal that you have set.

Setting unclear goals is not advisable because it will cause you to fumble around with what you want in your life. This happens due to the fact that you are never certain about what you want. The worst thing is that there is nothing that you will achieve which will impress you. There was nothing that you had set out to obtain. Accordingly, expect to get lost and settle for less.

Take an ordinary example of a weight-loss goal that one states because they simply want to shed some pounds. Yet, this goal is vague. You cannot envisage yourself on the other side of losing weight because you don't know how much you will be losing.

Challenge

Clarity is not the only ingredient that you require for your goal to be deemed effective. It is crucial to make sure that the goal you set is challenging. Why should your goal be challenging? You will gain nothing good by setting easy-to-achieve goals. In fact, you will only be lying to yourself. Conversely, challenging goals will bring a sense of accomplishment. As such, you will have a valid reason to celebrate.

Using the example of the weight-loss goal mentioned above, you will not feel excited if you lost three pounds in a span of three months. What this means is that you did not put in extra effort to lose weight. Your goals should drive you. They should be something worth sweating for. This is the best way for you to feel the joy of winning.

Commitment

The third principle, as proposed by Latham and Locke's theory, is commitment. It is vital that you show concern about what you are doing. When setting your goals, you shouldn't just set them for the sake of doing it. Rather, you ought to display some emotional commitment to what you are doing. As pointed out in the preceding principle, your goals should be challenging. This means that you will need some level of dedication to overcome these challenges. Without this, you will easily surrender on your mission.

Feedback

Goals also need reliable and consistent feedback. After setting your monthly goals, it is essential that you get feedback as to whether you are on track on not. In addition, feedback will give you some insight to understand what works and what doesn't. This allows you to polish your goals along the way to make sure that you focus on what you think will serve you best.

With reference to the example of losing weight, the last thing that you need is to find out two months later that your weight-loss plan didn't work. Ideally, the best strategy would be to gauge your performance weekly and find out the best exercises that will contribute to rapid weight loss. Therefore, feedback is highly important in goal setting.

Task complexity

Another principle that you should bear in mind when setting goals relates to task complexity. Sure, you will be setting a challenging goal to achieve. However, there is a trick that you can utilize to make sure that the goal is less challenging and attainable. This involves breaking down the bigger goal into smaller manageable goals. The advantage gained here is that you will feel that the task is less complex than it was before. You should avoid discouraging yourself in the process of trying to achieve your goals. For that reason, breaking down complex tasks comes highly recommended.

Setting SMART goals

As a means of ensuring that your goals meet the principles detailed in the preceding paragraphs, you ought to make sure that your goals are SMART goals. The term "SMART" is an acronym used to describe the aspects of a specified goal. A SMART goal is:

Specific

A good goal is specific. It should be clear-cut about what you want to achieve from your mission. What are you going to do? Setting specific goals will motivate you to find ideal ways of achieving them. To determine whether your goal is specific or not, you should be in a position to point out clearly what you expect to achieve.

Measurable

Can your goal be measured? Depending on how you are working toward your goal, it should be possible to track your progress. Through regular assessments, you will determine whether or not you are moving in the right direction. Take note of the fact that tracking your progress also provides feedback to make you aware of the tactics that work and those that don't. You can, therefore, adjust accordingly based on the results you get.

Achievable

It goes without saying that your goals should be achievable. In other words, they should be within your reach. Whether in business or in real life, the goals you set should be practical. In business, for example, you cannot set goals that demand a lot from your enterprise when you lack the required resources. Hence, your goals ought to be reasonable enough.

Relevant

This aspect relates to the notion of ensuring that your goals matter to you. They should reflect what you really want to achieve in life. It should drive you to the end of the tunnel where you realize your ambitions. In line with your personal goals, they should embody the type of person that you are. You cannot set personal goals that do not reflect who you are. As such, it is vital to make sure that your goals are not only realistic but also relevant.

Time-bound

So, you have set your goals and you are ready to put in effort toward achieving them. Well, before anything else, you should ask yourself whether you have a defined timeframe for achieving these goals. When are you going to complete your mission? Will you be done in a week, a month, or a year? Timely goals will guarantee that you prioritize your goals accordingly. This means that you will attend to more urgent matters first and schedule others for a more appropriate time.

Benefits of setting goals

From a general perspective, one would argue that goals help in giving people a direction in their lives. Of course, setting the right goals will guarantee that you make sound decisions that will ultimately bear a positive influence in your life. Take an ordinary example of a weekend that you failed to plan for. It is quite likely that you will spend time lazing around. Since you don't know what to do, you will feel bored. You will be ready to engage in any activity as long as it can keep you busy.

A reason to wake up every morning

Perhaps you have been feeling that your days are longer and that there is nothing serious to fill up your day's schedule. If you have been feeling this way, then most certainly you should set goals. Having a purpose to push toward will give you a reason to rise up early in the morning. People who have developed a habit of setting goals will attest to the fact that there are times when they can wake up without using their alarms. This is because the mind has been programmed to work and strive to meet set goals.

Get rid of distractions

Going through life without goals will also lead to many distractions. Usually, you will feel confused about what you should do. The moment anything comes along, you will not hesitate to jump into the wagon. Normally, this is not a trait that you would associate with successful people. They always have a goal to keep them focused throughout the year. Interestingly, sometimes they are too focused to spare some time to have fun. Eventually, their efforts pay off and they are the envy of society.

An opportunity to improve

Having goals also ensures that you improve in what you do. Setting clear and concise goals provides one with an opportunity to grow. You will wake up every morning striving to be the best version of yourself. Athletes are a good example of how goals can help you improve in what you are doing.

Athletes have goals that drive them to train every day. Their aim is to win competitions and all kinds of prizes that are ahead of them. This is what pushes them to train so that they can be the best at what they do.

Live your dreams

Set clear goals and you will live to see your dreams come true. With the constant motivation that will drive you toward your goal, there is nothing that will stop you from living the life that you have always yearned for. As such, goals not only motivate you, but they also provide you with a clear path toward success. Often, you will surround yourself with positive thoughts relating to your anticipated success. By the law of attraction, there is a guarantee that bliss will come your way.

Chapter 23

Forgetting Your Past

Getting rid of your junk

Another factor that contributes to our worry is our constant clutter in our closets and other places. When we have a lot of clutter in different places, we may become really stressed and overwhelmed by the amount of stuff that we have. But what if we could make it simpler? Why not get rid of the stuff that is holding us back from living a meaningful life? That is what this discussion is for—to show you how to get rid of your junk and live a minimalist lifestyle.

What if the new more is less? That is what the minimalists are saying. With more people graduating from four-year universities with student loan debts of more than $30,000 and people unable to get a decent job that pays the bills after graduating, it is no wonder that many millennials are in deep sludge. They cannot buy a car, let alone a house. Therefore, financially, it is becoming more difficult to be a millennial. Millennials are not likely to be able to retire later in their lives because of all the debt that they have acquired in their twenties. It makes for a difficult situation in every sense. The solution to all of this: buy less, consume less, and live with fewer possessions. That is what many millennials are having to do, and it is helping them to alleviate the worry of having so much junk that is causing many problems.

The key point to realize is that stuff does not make us happy. Accumulating more wealth, junk, and other material possessions is never going to make us happy. It is just going to make us more anxious about taking care of the things that could easily break, get damaged, or worse. We find ourselves worrying more when we have a mansion to take care of and other things. But as soon as we get rid of our junk, we find ourselves free to do greater things with our time. Miraculously, we are able to take a load off and stop worrying about the things that could go wrong or tear up. We also spend a lot more money this way, and we find ourselves unable to pay the bills each month, which is more disheartening and stressful.

What is the solution? Purge, purge, purge, I tell you! It is to get rid of everything that is getting in the way. That includes items that we absolutely do not need or desire. Don't let little things get in the way of your life. You should try to do everything to rid yourself of the things that are robbing you of joy at the end of the day because it is not worth it. Cast off everything that is causing you harm and anything that is unnecessary. You don't need it. Try to clean the house at least once a month. Take inventory of your needs and surpluses and then get rid of the things that are not part of your essential items. It will help you get to where you want to be.

Forgiving the past

Sometimes it can be hard to forgive people and situations that have hurt us deeply in the past. However, what we have to learn to do is to get over the past and discover ways to forgive the hurts that have caused us great trouble. We must think of ways to overcome our various situations and forgive the past.

It is easier said than done, I know. However, it is something that you have to do to get rid of the emotional and psychological baggage that you have in your life. Perhaps you have experienced a breakup with a person. It was a terrible experience for you; you are trying to figure out how to move on, but it is continually nagging at you. That's where you must learn to let go and forgive the past of the many things that you may have gone through and move on to the things that motivate you.

Forgiving past mistakes, misjudgments, and heartbreaks will give you the ability to overcome your fears and find peace within your soul. I'm sure that sometimes you feel troubled by the things happening in this world. There are things that can cause you anxiety and stress because they make you remember some childhood trauma or other difficult experiences in the past. When this happens, you begin to relive the painful things of the past.

You need to learn to forgive your past. It is not going to happen automatically. Often, forgiveness is a process that involves a great deal of time before you can carry it out. The only way to get over it is to forget about what happened. Granted, it may take you years to overcome the damage that someone has done in your life, and you may spend a lifetime trying to forgive them. However, the sooner you do that, the better off you will be.

There are many cases of people who have walked through life with the emotional baggage of childhood trauma. One such example was Robin

Williams, who had a lonely childhood. His parents put him in an attic of the house, where he was forced to play with his toys all by himself. He rarely saw his parents, except during private dinner gatherings. In that case, Robin felt that he was constantly seeking the validation and love of other people. Many people loved Robin, and they showed it, but he struggled to love himself because he had not felt that as a child. Consequently, he went through his life, struggling with the concept of love because his parents had not shown him love. That deep sadness followed him all the way to his grave after his suicide in 2014.

What Robin Williams shows us is an example of someone who had childhood worries and challenges follow him throughout his life. He was never able to forgive and forget the past, even though it would have helped him to live a more fulfilling life. We can learn from this example that childhood anxieties and trauma can follow us well into adulthood and that if we are not careful, they may follow us all the way to our death. It can be difficult to articulate our concerns to people because they are buried deep within us. Inside our psychology, there are hurting children who are struggling to overcome the difficulties of the past, but the sooner we can overcome the past, the sooner we will be happy and able to live a life that is full of love, joy, peace, and good fortune.

Another example of a person who released the past hurt was Will Hunting from Good Will Hunting (1997), a movie with Ben Affleck, Matt Damon, and Robin Williams. Matt Damon's character, Will, is the main character who has been hurting from his past because he was abandoned by his parents and lived a life as an orphan with no family.

He tried to mask his insecurities by drinking, smoking cigarettes, and using physical violence against others. However, he met Dr. Maguire, a psychologist who was played by Robin Williams. The psychologist was able to connect with Will on a deep emotional level and provide him the support he needed to overcome his past trauma. In one emotionally gripping moment, Robin Williams was able to get all the hurt out of Matt Damon's character as he burst into tears and hugged him. To calm him down, Robin's character, Maguire, kept saying, "It is not your fault." It was helpful to see this moment because it showed that the past could be effectively forgiven and wiped clean if a person wanted to do that. Maguire was able to get the pain out of Will and bring him to the point of forgiving the past. Although he might never forget what his parents had done to him to abuse him and eventually leave him, Will would be able to move on and do what he was meant to do, which was to "go and see about a girl." The touching story showed us how the past could be erased so that a person could go forward and discover his destiny. With moments of healing and wholeness, Will would be able to leave behind the darkness of his past and pursue his dream of being in love with someone.

What can we do to forgive our own past? The important thing to do is to realize that we need healing—spiritual, mental, and physical healing. Our minds and hearts are not in the right place. We have hurt from the past, and we feel that it is a dark chasm that we cannot escape from. However, we have to bring ourselves to repenting of our own misjudgments and the things that have caused us pain and anxiety and then also forgive those around us who have hurt us in some way. It is not easy, but it is a path that is well worth it because then we can find a way to feel better and heal. It is a lifelong process in some cases, but as we get rid of our excess emotional baggage, then we can find a freer and more prosperous future in our minds. It is crucial that we release stress, anxiety, and other things that are holding us back. If we don't do that, then we may be holding to something for the rest of our lives that could ultimately lead to our own downfall and destruction, as in the case of Robin Williams. Let's look at the ways that we can do this. How can we emotionally release the past from our hearts and minds?

Practical applications

1. Write down all the things that are causing us anxiety and worry and leave them for later. We should allow ourselves to release all the pain into the paper. After that, you burn the paper, shred it, or do anything to it to show that it is gone forever.

2. Say you're sorry to people you have hurt. What you have to do with this application is to say sorry to people whom you may have caused pain and anxiety. You may not realize how much this has put a rift in your relationship, and you will have to take the initiative to do it because it is highly likely the other person will not take the first step. You have to be proactive about this point.

3. Keep yourself super busy with things that you won't have time to worry or dwell on the past. You should find some ways to keep yourself busy so that you won't think about the things of the past. Do many kinds of projects that will help you experience joy and meaning in your life? Do things that give you passion.

4. Spend time with the people you love and don't spend time with negative people. Another point that you should think about is spending time with people who give you joy and avoiding Negative Nancy and other people who will just bring you down. This will help you to live a happier life.

Chapter 24

Deliberate Thinking

To do something deliberately is to do it with intention. Deliberate thinking, then, is quite simply the act of thinking thoughts with deliberate intent. Very often, individuals can feel as if they have no control over plaguing thoughts. It is as if these thoughts come into your line of focus and demand your time and energy like bullies or authorities that are out of one's power to control. This is not necessarily an exaggeration. If we do not practice keeping our thoughts in check, they will start to bully us and it can feel futile to try to cast those thoughts aside. They are so loud and so aggressive that we feel it is necessary to focus on the thought now and until it is resolved.

In reality, this is a choice.

The average individual is capable of navigating and managing thoughts of their own accord, but it is the lack of practice doing so that makes it feel useless. If you have never driven a car before, it does not mean you are incapable of driving; it means you have not been taught to drive. If your intention is to truly get a grip on overthinking, then you can do this with the practice of deliberate thinking. When you notice thoughts beginning to demand more of your time and attention than feels good to give it now that is the perfect time to practice deliberate thinking, rather than allowing your thoughts to run wild and unchecked. This is an opportunity to reclaim more power and influence over the outcomes and results you see in your daily life.

When you practice deliberate thinking, it means taking responsibility for what happens in your life; for what will happen in your future. You cannot ask for your power back only to relinquish it when something undesirable happens to you. You cannot take responsibility for the goodness that is coming to you, and leave the responsibility of the discomfort. You are responsible for it all, or you are under the control of external elements of which you surely have no control.

If you accept this responsibility, it means you no longer blame other people and other circumstances for your position. You have, in one way or another, brought the position to yourself. It may feel uncomfortable to accept that you are primarily the cause of your own discomfort. However, if you are brave enough to accept this, it comes with incomparable freedom. If you are responsible for all that has come, then you are responsible for all that will come. If you learn to effectively use tools like the power of positive thinking and the power of deliberate thinking, and then you are free to sculpt whatever future you desire.

Deliberate thinking, like positive thinking, is more about a change in attitude than anything else is. It is about the deliberate intent to train yourself for better thinking, and better-feeling thoughts. When something happens that is not in alignment with that goal, it is your job as a positive, deliberate thinker, to change your perspective on the subject, or to acknowledge its presence and dismiss it from your attention promptly. This doesn't mean ignoring the issue altogether, it means dismissing it until it feels good to work with it, think about it, and figure it out.

There may be a subject that feels big, scary, and uncomfortable. It has been buzzing around you for a while now. It calls on your attention and demands your focus even when you do not intend to be thinking about it. The thought creeps in as you are working or as you are attempting to enjoy the company of a friend. It stomps and shouts at you and demands your attention, growing louder and more unruly by the minute. It is ok to dismiss that thought for now, even if the subject is something you certainly must confront. However, chances are you do not have to give your attention to it at this very moment. Practice dismissing those unruly thoughts and send them back to the waiting room. Eventually, you will regain a reasonable degree of confidence and power over your habits of thought, and it will, at some point, actually feel good to deal with and resolve the tormenting issue. Rather than fight with oneself, the deliberate thinker practices control and dominance over thought; dismissing the situation from focus, for the time being.

How to use deliberate thinking with positive thinking?

The combination of positive thinking and deliberate thinking is unbeatable and this is a major factor for the insight and focus on this book. These are your two most powerful weapons and there is nothing you cannot confront without them. These tools remind you that you have the power and you are in control. Not necessarily control of all worldly circumstances, but rather, how you react to them.

If deliberate thinking is to think with intent, this could, in theory, mean the intention of dwelling in uncomfortable, bad-feeling thoughts. Deliberate means intentional; not necessarily good. To practice intentionally, but without the benefit of positive thought, could land you in a similar or worse nightmare of overthinking.

Positive thinking without deliberate thinking is a pattern with no goal or destination; no sense of accomplishment. It can be easy to float through the day enjoying every butterfly and rainbow, but without intention behind your patterns of thought and behavior, there is little to be gained. Overthinkers generally want to regain control over their thoughts in order to accomplish something; a series of things. Happy thoughts without direction may feel good, but your train will be headed to an unknown destination. If that is your intention, so be it, but many of us have other intentions in mind and this will be most easily accomplished by a combination of deliberate and positive thinking.

Pros and Cons of Positive and Deliberate Thinking

It is possible for someone to fall into positive thinking but end up misunderstanding it and misusing it. These individuals can dig themselves even deeper into discomfort. Therefore, it is highly recommended that you familiarize yourself with some of the most common advantages and disadvantages of employing this method of positive thought modification. Let us assess the following list so you know what to watch out for and what to look forward to.

Disadvantages of Positive and Deliberate Thinking

1. Only positive thoughts - Eradicating all "negative" thought can be detrimental to the individual. Some of the thought processes referred to as negative actually helpful and beneficial to us. Considering a worst-case scenario can help us to plan and prepare for an outcome so that the impact is not felt so harshly. Emotions like fear and worry can, in some cases, protect us from dangerous circumstances. It is important to accept this as part of your repertoire and rather than see this as a negative, consider it a positive thought-behavior. However, do not let this thinking spiral out of control. There is a difference between mitigating damages by considering worst-case scenarios and stewing over worst-case scenarios for an excessive amount of time, or in a way, that exhausts you.

2. Ignore real life - It is possible to become so enamored with the idea of positive thinking that the individual may begin to ignore primary concerns. While it should be your priority to think about that, which feels good, it does not mean you should neglect important aspects of day-to-day life. Neglecting that which needs your attention does not actually feel good anyway. It may be a delay in dealing with those uncomfortable feelings, but you still know in your mind and in your heart, those issues are there and they need your attention. If you find yourself having to confront an uncomfortable circumstance, as a positive thinker, you do not mindlessly ignore it. Instead, you acknowledge its existence and make a deliberate decision to confront the issue now, or at a better time in the near future.

3. Positive Thinking as your only tool - While positive and deliberate thinking can be a powerful tool for thinkers, it is important to recognize that is not the only tool you have. Becoming overly reliant on this one method of thinking and behavior actually creates another automatic response for your mind and body to follow whether or not it is actually the best course of thought and action. You end up in a spot much as you started in, where your actions and thoughts are rote, mechanical, and not deliberate.

4. Judgment from others - Just because you're at a point in your life where making positive and deliberate changes to your thought- and behavior-patterns feels good, doesn't mean everyone around you is ready for it. Be as gentle with others as you are with yourself and do not expect others to fall in line and think positively along with you. Often times, this journey is one you make on your own. It is unfair to expect someone else to adapt so quickly.

5. Removing yourself from the fuss - This can be a difficult step to cross over because we are, largely, social creatures. We want to express and share. However, a brief looks around you will demonstrate that a great many conversations taking place are neither positive nor deliberate. Spending 45 minutes arguing politics online with another person is likely not part of your deliberate goal. By giving your attention to this debate, you are likely slowing down your train by conjuring feelings of frustration, helplessness, and even anger. This can send your train jolting the wrong direction down a negative path.

6. Self-punishment - It can be a natural reaction for many Overthinkers to punish themselves mentally, emotionally, even physically, when they find themselves slipping up and letting the negative train build momentum again. Do not punish yourself. You have not done anything wrong. Allowing the mind to naturally swing back to uncomfortable thoughts is absolutely part of the process. To be mad at yourself for slipping back is equivalent to the carpenter who hammers one nail into the wood and becomes mad that not all nails were hammered into the wood at that moment.

Advantages of positive and deliberate thinking

The advantages of positive and deliberate thinking are more obvious and easier to see than perhaps the disadvantages are. By now, you should have some idea that positive and deliberate thinking yields highly beneficial results, especially when employed by Overthinkers. Here are some of the most beneficial rewards:

- A sense of clarity and clear thought

- The power to acknowledge and dismiss thoughts without guilt or delay

- The decrease in stress, which plays an enormous part in how the body physically feels and reacts

- Lower rates of depression

- Greater resistance to immune-system illnesses

- Greater self-worth

- Higher levels of confidence

- Self-accomplishment and self-actualization

- A better general mood and attitude

- A sense of well-being and everything in its place

- A certainty that you can handle life's circumstances in a healthy way

- Your healthy practice becomes a model for others to follow

- Gained control over thought-patterns

- Removal of automatic responses that are no longer serving you

- Removal of harmful behaviors that are no longer in alignment with your deliberate goal to feel good.

Chapter 25

Exercises That Help Positive Thinking

Positive thinking is a good habit and like any good habit it takes time to inculcate. Here are a few simple and very effective exercises and methods that will help you to think positive – no matter what.

Getting rid of worrying

What is worrying? Worrying is misplaced imagination. The problem with worrying is that it has the power to stress you to no end–for no actual reason because in majority of cases nothing happens. When you worry, you think about the possibilities of things going wrong.

You need to get rid of worrying. To do so, instead of worrying prepare for the worst possible scenario. Think beforehand, "What could go wrong here?" and prepare for any of those eventualities. Worry comes when you are not prepared well enough because it makes you feel helpless to the outcome.

Counter the helpless feeling by preparing for all possible mishaps that could be controlled. The rest you leave to the eventualities of life, what will be will be. Accept that you cannot control everything no matter what you do. So, give your best possible shot and leave the rest to fate.

Side by side, ensure that you have enough to occupy your mind when you think you are prone for a worry attack. If you have something to do, it is least likely that you will worry too much. Do something pleasant and happy–preferably for someone else.

No complaints for 24 hours

Have a "24-hours of no complaints" period as often as you can in your schedule. You could have it once a month or once a week. When this period is declared, the rule would be that you cannot complain about anything you find annoying, no matter what. Instead, try looking beyond it and do something constructive.

A nice story can give you a fair idea of how useful this method can be. A lady was shopping at a supermarket and observed that the cashier was very grumpy. She was snappy bordering on rude. The people she served responded with equal or more irritation.

When this lady's turn came, the cashier almost threw her change on the counter. However, the lady did not take offence; instead, she smiled at the cashier and asked her full of empathy, "You had a rough day dear, didn't you?" Then, paying her a tip she said, "Here dear have a wonderful cup of coffee on me. It will make you feel better."

Surprisingly, the cashier smiled, accepted the tip and said, "Thank you so much. My daughter is in the hospital and I could not get off today. I am very upset. Thank you for understanding."

Very often giving the benefit of doubt is all it takes to make the day better for you and others. Unfortunately, we tend to jump to the worst conclusions when we should rather be a little empathic. Next time, when you feel like snapping a biting retort to someone rude, take a deep breath, count to 10 and reply with kindness. It will definitely make your day because you refused to allow the incident to make you angry; and it may change that person's day for the better, too.

3-6 Hours of pure kindness

Another way to make you feel good and encourage positive thinking is to give yourself a 3-6 hours' time out when you should be kind to everyone around you. Be warned that this could be stressful initially, because you cannot get angry with anyone or say an unkind word, or do anything unkind to anyone – no matter what.

The greatest gift you can give yourself and others is compassion. When you impose these hours of pure kindness, you will learn to see the good in every person. It is impossible to get angry with anyone if and when you see the good in them.

Like the example in the "cashier lady" story, you need to understand that when someone behaves badly it is because that person is unhappy for some reason. This person needs your compassion the most. If you practice kindness in spite of the response, you will realize that this helps you more than the recipient.

Kindness – when offered unconditionally - has the power to calm your mind and fill you with a tranquility that is beyond compare.

Thank you, I appreciate it very much

Learn to appreciate others. Say "thank you" as often as you can; say it with genuineness and feeling. Everybody loves to be appreciated for what they do. It is wonderfully rewarding and motivating to receive a well said "thank you." Whenever somebody does you a good turn, no matter how small be quick to say, "thank you."

Learning to appreciate others will make it easier to appreciate the good things in your life. Every person has a long list of blessings, happy hours, good times – but we tend to focus on the negative–what we do not have, what we lost, what we would have had and lose the chance to enjoy what we DO have.

Whether you say, "thank you" to God, your friend, your spouse, your children, a stranger or anyone who did something for you, the benefit of it comes to you first. When you say "thank you" you realize that you received something nice and you have a reason to be happy.

Learnt to be grateful for what you have and say it aloud as often as you can. Say "thank you" as often as you can. It will make you happy.

Sorry, I hurt you – please forgive me

Just as it is important to say, "thank you," it is important to say "sorry" as often as it is required and with genuine feelings. Whenever you realize you have hurt anyone, be quick to express your remorse. Say "sorry" as soon as you can. This will clear the air and allow healing on both sides.

An apology put forth appropriately will always create positive energy. Try this experiment. Next time when you are in an angry altercation with anyone, take a deep breath and say, "I am sorry if what I did (or said) hurt you." See what happens. In most cases, when you say you're sorry the anger dissipates like smoke.

With the anger gone, good vibes come right back in and you will be surprised how good it feels for you as well.

It's okay, I forgive you

It is important that you can forgive those who hurt you as well. Often, we carry a grudge forever, without realizing that the anger and hurt erodes the soul and mind. Revenge is a poison that you carry inside you. When you hold anything against a person who has hurt you, you are tying yourself to that person and reliving the hurt again and again.

Forgiving means letting the bitterness go, which in turn sets you free. All religions advocate forgiveness—with a good reason. When you forgive, you become emotionally free of pain. Try it; you will feel a weight lifted off your shoulders, literally. It is a wonderful feeling to let go of the hurt. Forgiveness is a gift you offer yourself more than the others.

Chapter 26

How to Make Important Decisions Today?

When it comes to making these important decisions without delay, there are a few strategies that may help you out. Many of us are so swamped with work and other stressors in our life that we often fail to realize how easy it often is to simplify more complex situations and processes, in order to make an important decision.

Decisions always have an impact on something, but the impact is not always at the same level. Sometimes, a decision may affect how you feel, such as when you decide not to pack lunch for the day. Often, such a small decision would not have a major impact on your life–you can go to the cafeteria and buy something to eat when you feel hungry or during your lunch hour.

Other times, however, decisions have a much larger impact–such as when you have to make a choice that could mean a client would sign a contract with your firm or rather go to another firm. This can be a major loss, especially when the client would be worth millions to your company, should you make the wrong choice and the client goes with their second choice.

The more of an impact a decision will have, the more you would have to consider the different options and ensure that the one you choose will have a most positive impact on your life or your career, compared to the other options that are available to choose from.

Know your goals

Prior to making a decision that will have an impact on your life or your career, such as those that may result in a hire from a client, it is vital that you completely understand the goals that you are trying to reach with the particular decision that hangs on your shoulders. Understand exactly what needs to be done with that decision.

For example, is your goal to buy a new house? Understand the smaller goals involved as well. When you are trying to buy a house, you want to ensure there is adequate room for your family, so your goal will be to buy a house that has enough rooms, as well as living space, to accommodate everyone. You also have the goal of choosing a house that is close to schools and to your workplace and that of your wife.

At work, you might need to make a decision on a specific client as there is a conflict between two that you can sign. While the primary goal would be to make money through signing one of these clients, another goal may be to sign the one that could provide your business with a longer-term relationship and projects that will last for several years, even if it means a slightly lower profit on the first project compared to the other client.

Be prepared and well-informed

You should be well-informed and very much prepared in order to make a decision that will be best for you, your family, or your business, depending on which party the decision will have an effect on. Thus, always ensure that you obtain as much information as possible related to a project, or whatever it is that is involved before you decide on which option you choose.

The same goes for a business-related decision. Have interviews with the clients that will be affected by your decision. Ask the right questions. Know what they expect. Know what needs to be done. Understand what is involved.

All this information will help you filter out the bad options and choose the option that is best suited for the current scenario.

Make a biased decision

It is okay to listen to that gut feeling you get sometimes and to hear out the opinions of other people in your life, whether colleagues, family members, or friends, but it is also important that the decision you made is biased. Even though many would advise being unbiased, I personally find that making decisions in favor of something or someone, such as the parties involved in the situation, really is the best way to go about a decision-making process, and ultimately to avoid constantly finding yourself making delay after delay.

Consider the parties involved and understand what would be considered in their favor when making the final decision. Perhaps your family prefers a dog, so opt for a house with a big yard as compared to a smaller yard or an apartment in a more convenient location – that would be a biased decision based on the preferences of your family.

Weigh out all the pros and cons

Each of the options that you can choose from when you make an important decision has pros and cons involved. It might not always be easy to identify all of the pros and all of the potential drawbacks related to a particular option, but setting up a list of what you know would happen, how you, your family, or perhaps your business could benefit, and what the downsides will be, can be a big help and will ensure making that decision becomes much easier in the end.

Make a list with all the options that are available. Then, set up a sub-list beneath each one. Write down some of the pros and then write down a couple of cons. Be realistic when you write down these factors. Consider all the research that has been done, the information you have gathered, and take the other points I have covered here into account as well.

When you look back at the list you made, you will start to get a better picture of which decision or option is the better choice to make, when comparing the pros and cons of each option in front of you.

Understand possible consequences and complications

Actions have consequences. Sometimes, even making the right decision in life can pose a threat to someone or to some party, and possibly lead to a series of complications. This is why making a list of pros and cons that can be associated with each option you are facing is often not enough. Additionally, you need to consider the chain of reactions that may occur once you make the decision – you need to do this for each of the options that you have listed.

If you choose a house with a bigger yard instead of an apartment in town, then you might have to drive a long way to drop off the kids at school and to get to the office. The reaction here would be the longer distance, which means a longer driving time in the morning and in the afternoon. In turn, you will have to get up earlier and perhaps move faster in the morning. This will also push up your monthly expenses for gas. Your car may need more regular services if you are going to be driving longer distances.

The same type of thought should go into decisions that will affect your career and the company you work at, whether you own the company or simply serve as an employee. If you are going to sign one client over another client, due to a conflict of interest or another related matter, then you need to consider possible consequences that may arise when you choose one particular client. If you need to select a venue, consider possible complications that may arise with each of the options.

Time for action

After you have done thorough planning, you know the pros and cons of every option in front of you, and you should have an idea of the decision you need to make. Things should be much simpler now and give you the opportunity to make the decision without further delay.

When it is time for action, make the decision. Don't delay again. You have all the information and data that you now need to make the right decision and choose the option that will be most suited to the current situation. Take action, make the decision, and follow the appropriate procedures in order to follow through on that particular decision that you have decided to make.

Following up on your action

This is a step that people usually overlook and, while it is not really a necessity, I highly suggest that you take a moment to reflect on those decisions that you have made. Consider how they have worked out. I personally take 20 minutes once a week in order to follow up on the decisions that I have made during the week. I do this on the weekend when things are calmer. I sit down and take a look at all my notes related to any important decisions that I made. I consider the options I had, and how the one that I ended up choosing affected the particulars and parties involved.

This way, you will be able to learn from your own mistakes and motivate yourself through those decisions that worked out perfectly. Congratulate yourself on successful choices. Don't scold yourself on those that didn't work out great – rather look at why they didn't work out and see what you could have done differently. This way, you can avoid making such mistakes again in the future.

When is it better to delay a decision?

I know I just gave you the old speech of never delaying a decision and to stop procrastinating, but I do want to touch a quick topic – sometimes, in rare cases, it might be better to delay the process of choosing between different options. It is, however, essential that you understand that this only accounts for special cases and the fact that I am suggesting a possible delay should not give you the opportunity to make excuses when your case does not meet the criteria I am going to discuss here.

First of all, if the decision that you have to make is small and will have no significant impact on your life or in the workplace, then don't delay. No matter how small, the fact that you still need to make that decision will linger in your mind and add to the clutter that may already be present.

For small decisions, consider your options, weigh the pros and cons of each option, and then decide.

When the decision you have to make will have a bigger impact, however, then there are cases where you might want to consider a small delay. At the same time, I want to stress the fact that delaying should not lead to further delaying! One single delay and then, when the time comes, you need to make a choice.

The only time when important decisions should really be delayed is in cases where you feel sick or very tired. For example, if you have caught the flu or you have stayed up all night working on a project. Such scenarios call for rest and healing. ONLY delay the decision up to the time when you have gotten some sleep or when the flu has passed, then immediately start to work on a plan-of-action to ensure you can choose the most appropriate option.

Conclusion

It's so incredibly important to not only be comfortable with yourself as it pertains to healing yourself and the people around you while you go through that journey but to be able to actively make your life happier as you go through it. Often, you develop a lot of anxiety as a result of negative emotions or simply a lack of emotion. The apathy we feel is a direct derivative of anxiety, and we overthink because our brain doesn't have any emotions to focus on, so it creates its own out of anxiety, stress, and apathy.

The most relevant part of healing is having those positive emotions brought back so that you give yourself positive experiences without the need to stress yourself out unnecessarily. For example, going outside and disconnecting from your devices for a little while can go a long way in stimulating positive emotions. We feel good when we go outside and smell the fresh air, and we feel good when we feel the most connected to the ground beneath us. Because being outside stimulates this kind of very basic pleasure in us, you should seek it out when you can. This doesn't have to be a part of your regimen, which you keep up with daily, but you should go outside fairly often so that you can really experience the real world around you for what it is in a basic, carnal way. Going outside doesn't have to be a solitary experience, either. It can be relaxing and cathartic to just take a walk outside with friends or other loved ones. It helps you not only to calm down, but it can be a good way for you to talk plainly with the people you care about and who care about you. Letting them into your life in a more honest and up-front way is a good venue for you to be happier in the long run. Being in nature tends to have this effect on people—we feel calmer and more emotionally stable and relaxed when we're outside, so it makes sense that we might be more willing to reach out to people and talk with them honestly about their lives, how they feel, as well as our own experiences with them. Having these experiences mesh together over a length of time can be incredibly healing for everyone involved.

When you feel overwhelmed with the pressures of life, and you feel as though you might collapse under the weight of your own stresses, it's a good time to step back and have an in-depth look at why you are where you are and why you're doing what you're doing. Assess yourself and your position at the moment and determine how important that position is to you. Your mental and emotional health should always come before the wants of others and what they might demand from you. If there's someone in your life who's asking something of you and it would just be too much, you have the ability and the freedom to decline in an exercise of putting yourself first. Often, a lot of your stress arises from not knowing how to prioritize yourself above other people. When we learn this irreplaceable skill, we become aware of our place with our friends and loved ones and we understand better how we can make ourselves and our lives happier. If you're in a place or position where you don't feel happy, get out of that situation. You aren't being terrible or selfish for wanting the best for yourself and wanting to be happy for the sake of being happy. Even if you don't want people to view you as selfish, there are more important things in your life than pleasing others instead of pleasing yourself. Be hedonistic on an intimate, spiritual level. There are ways that you can please yourself on the level of the emotions and the brain which you might not have been able to do or work up the courage to commit to before you started trying to undo all the trauma done to you over time. Indulge in something you enjoy now and then, splurge on something you've had your eye on for a while, turn down plans if you don't feel like going out, and have days to yourself where you can just sit back, relax, and enjoy your own company in a way that you might not be able to if there was anyone else around, no matter how close to you they were. When we prioritize ourselves and learn to simply cut our losses emotionally, we free ourselves to so many healing experiences we would never have had if we didn't know how to make those changes and make decisions for the sake of our mental health instead of for the sake of the happiness of other people. Even so much as taking a day off from your obligations if you can, and having just an afternoon where you can indulge and treat yourself can be an incredibly healing experience in and of itself. Indulging yourself and accepting yourself as someone who needs to be cared for and loved, even if it has to be by you, can bring you so much joy and emotional release that you might never have had access to otherwise.

Ultimately, there might be people in your life who are preventing you from being this best version of yourself. These people are toxic people, and they might be involved in any part of your life. They might be your friends, your family, your coworkers, or anyone else in your support system, or out of it, who you talk to regularly and who are having a direct negative impact on your life. Toxic people can look at any range of ways, and they come in many disguises. You might have been a toxic person at one point—most people have toxic traits or traits in their personality, which could be improved to make them more pleasant to be around and healthy for themselves and for others. Regardless of whether or not you have toxic traits now or did before, that doesn't mean you can't be affected by them in other people today. The more you learn about people in your life, the more easily you might begin to see them for what they truly are. If you know a toxic person in your life, you'll likely know by the way they act before the way they look. Toxic people tend to manipulate others in order to get what they want, and they don't tend to feel a lot of remorse when they successfully manipulate other people into doing what they need them to do. Toxic people get other, submissive people to do their dirty work for them while they sit back and manipulate everyone else behind the scenes. Toxic people might have very depressive actions, they might be anxious, they might be narcissistic, they could have any number of symptoms of other mental illnesses or signs that they aren't all there or they have plans and abilities to manipulate you to get what they want and think they deserve. You have probably been manipulated by a toxic person at some point in the last month or two. You also probably have at least one person in your life who would be considered toxic. Consider if someone you know or someone even in your support system has ever used the powers of eloquence and their own words against you to blackmail you or guilt you into being in emotional debt to them. Do they hold grudges against you for things that happened ages ago and might not have even been your fault? Do they have any way of guilting you or gaslighting you by playing the victim until you give in to their rhetoric and do what they want? If this is the case, you're dealing with a toxic manipulator and you can free up your life and your soul if you drop them as quickly as you can. Once you eliminate them from your life, you can feel yourself healing from all the bad energy that was with you with that person. Don't think of it as a major loss if you lose them for good—manipulators tend to be dramatic and make large shows out of abandoning people and making them feel pretty difficult. When we do knock them down, they might try to re-enter or take advantage of other people or things in our lives, so we don't force them out. This can be incredibly disturbing, so always have a way you can protect yourself and other people from people like this who are potentially dangerous or obsessive. The point of cutting off dangerous or otherwise very toxic people is not to put you in danger or even to stand up for what is right. You should want to cut off people who make you sad and angry—people who make your life less enjoyable to live every day and people you have lost your precious time for having to take care of them and cater to them. You drop toxic people for no one else's sake but your own, no matter what.

That is the nature of toxic people and removing them from your life. When you initially take them out, it feels as though something is gone, wrong, or missing. However, as time goes on and the hole begins to close, we often realize the hole should never have existed in the first place. Something new and better and healthy might have even begun to sprout in its place. If this is the case, be sure to foster whatever is growing anew. It might be something healthy that will enrich your experience and help you to be happier overall. It might be something toxic that is growing in that place of its toxic parent, in which case you can nip toxic behavior in the bud before it gets too bad.

When we overthink, it feels as though it controls our lives. Every move we make and every thought we have feels as though it's already been governed by this force in our head, which tells us that no matter what, we'll fail. No matter what we'll feel worthless, we'll never succeed no matter what, and so on and so forth. This impact can be damaging, not only to our professional career but also to our intimate, personal lives. The way being constantly told we don't meet some kind of invisible standard and never will as a kid messes with you in a way that is incomparable to many other experiences you can have while growing up. However, while you grow up, reflect on who got you there. You are always growing up, no matter how old you are, so always assess yourself and reflect on how you did today and how you did tomorrow. When you're constantly self-assessing in a way that is constructive, you can get so much done and quickly become the best version of yourself. Being aware of yourself, your emotions, and your mind is the best way that you can stay on track and make sure you become the best person you can be.

Made in the USA
Coppell, TX
29 January 2025